Questions
Children Ask

by EDITH and ERNEST BONHIVERT

revised in consultation with DR. MURIEL STANEK, Chicago Public Schools

illustrations by Helen Endres, John Faulkner, Joseph Rogers,
Dan Siculan, and George Suyeoka

Managing Editor ANNE NEIGOFF

STANDARD EDUCATIONAL CORPORATION

Chicago 1981

We wish to express our appreciation
to the many people who have helped in the
preparation of *Questions Children Ask*. We
are especially grateful for the assistance
of the following in planning, testing,
or authenticating this material:

Kenneth E. Howe, PH.D., Director of the
Children's School, National College of
Education, Evanston.

Bertha Morris Parker, assisted by Barbara
Wehr, Bryan Swan, and Richard Smith,
Science Department of the Laboratory
School, University of Chicago.

Wayne J. Rohse, M.D., The Stritch School
of Medicine, Loyola University, Chicago.

Ardo Luisado, M.D., Chief of the Cardiology
Department, Mt. Sinai Hospital, Chicago.

Emmet R. Blake, Curator of Birds, and
Colin C. Sanborn, Curator of Mammals,
Chicago Natural History Museum.

Art Direction and Design: Willis Proudfoot

Standard Book Number 87392-006-6

To
Boys and Girls
Everywhere

This is your book. You children asked the questions. That is why we call this book *Questions Children Ask*.

You asked many, many questions. We kept a Question Box into which we put all the questions that came to us through the mail or over the telephone. Into the box went the questions you children asked us and the questions you asked your mothers or fathers or teachers.

Each day we emptied the Question Box and looked at your questions. You asked all kinds! How does a spaceman walk in space? Why do leaves turn red and yellow in fall? How does television work?

Have you asked any of those questions? Do you know the answers?

Do you know what questions you asked most often? There were many questions about yourself, your home, and your school. You asked about puppies and bears and dinosaurs. You asked whether plants ever sleep. You asked why the sky is blue and why the tides come in and go out. You wanted to know about jet planes and submarines, too, and what kinds of work people do at an airport and at a newspaper and what a fireman does.

You asked how popcorn pops and why we dress up as witches and ghosts and goblins on Halloween.

These are just some of the questions you asked.

Many people helped us find the answers. Now you can read the answers in your book, *Questions Children Ask*. You can see the answers, too, in the exciting, colorful pictures.

We hope you'll keep on asking many more questions. We hope, too, that you will discover it's fun to find answers of your own!

Contents

Children Ask
About Themselves

I wonder why

—I can see red balloons, blue, yellow, green, and orange balloons. I see big things, little things, round, square, and pointed things, too.

—I can hear planes roaring, boys whistling, whispers, shouts.

—I can smell cookies baking, burning leaves, sweet and spicy smells, flower smells, and gasoline.

—I can taste hamburgers, marshmallows, salty peanuts, lemonade, hot chocolate, ice cream, and gingerbread.

—I can touch smooth pebbles, furry kittens, squashy mud, and wet snow.

—I can step up and down in the dark.

—I can tiptoe and slide and jump rope and turn somersaults.

—I can talk and sing and laugh and cry.

—I can ask questions.

—*I wonder why!*

What am I made of?

When you look into a mirror, you can see yourself. You can see your face, your hair, your arms and legs, your skin. But inside of you, there are many other parts you cannot see. You have bones, muscles, and blood. You have a brain, lungs, heart, stomach, and many other parts.

Every part of your body—the parts you can see and the parts you cannot see—is made up of cells. These cells are so tiny that you can see them only under a microscope. There are millions and millions of these tiny cells in your body. Each part of your body has its own special kind of cells. Bone cells do not look like skin cells. Muscle cells do not look like blood cells. There are special kinds of cells for seeing and special cells for tasting. Each kind of cell has its own work to do.

All the cells in your body work together to make up you!

How do I grow?

You grow because the cells in your body grow and make new cells. Because the cells are alive, they need food to help them grow. After you eat food, it is digested and carried by the blood to the tiny cells in all parts of your body.

Each tiny cell grows. When it is fully grown, it divides into two new cells. These new cells grow and divide and make four new cells. This growing and dividing goes on and on. That is how you grow bigger and taller.

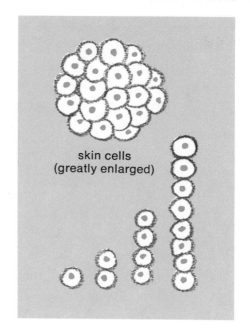

skin cells
(greatly enlarged)

When will I stop growing?

You will keep growing like this until you reach your full size. Girls usually do not grow taller after they are eighteen years old. Boys may keep growing taller for a few more years. When you are grown up, just enough new cells keep growing to take the place of older cells that wear out and die. New cells are always taking the place of old cells that die.

When you skin your knee, you scrape off many skin cells. But the skin cells around the sore spot keep growing and dividing. Soon new skin covers the skinned place on your knee. Next time you skin your knee, watch and see what happens.

How can I grow tall and strong?

Your cells need food to grow. They need food to make energy, too, so you can run and jump and work and play. Eating the right kinds of foods will help you grow tall and strong.

Your body needs protein to make new cells. Milk, eggs, meat, fish, peas, and nuts are some of the foods that give you protein.

Your body needs carbohydrates to give you energy. Potatoes, fruit, cereal, and corn are some of the energy foods which give you these carbohydrates.

Your body needs some fats, too. They help build energy and they also help you store away food in your body for later use. Some of the foods rich in fats are milk, butter, meat, and ice cream.

Your body also needs vitamins and minerals to give you strong bones and teeth. Foods that have vitamins and minerals are milk, green vegetables, and liver.

To grow tall and strong, you should eat the right kinds of food. But you also need fresh air and exercise and plenty of sleep and rest. And you need soap and water, for when you keep your body clean, you are helping to make it healthy and strong.

Why can't I eat only what I like?

What do you like best to eat? Is it ice cream and candy? Can you guess what would happen if you ate only ice cream and candy for breakfast, lunch, and dinner? Soon you would feel cross and tired and probably you would have a stomach ache! Your body needs many kinds of foods to keep you strong and healthy. And can you guess what else would happen if you ate only ice cream and candy? Soon you would be tired of them and they would no longer taste as good! You enjoy food best when you try many kinds of foods with many kinds of tastes. Try it and see.

How can a baby live only on milk?

A tiny baby does not have teeth to bite and chew foods, but he needs food to make him grow. He needs food to give him energy. Milk gives him this food for in milk are proteins, carbohydrates, fats, vitamins, and minerals. After a few weeks, the baby begins to eat other foods that give him the things he needs that are not in milk. At first he eats only a few spoonfuls a day of soft foods like baby cereal.

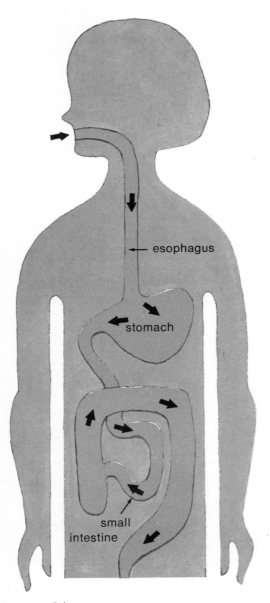

esophagus

stomach

small
intestine

What happens to the food I eat?
Inside your body, the food you eat has to be changed, or digested, so it can pass into your blood and travel to all parts of your body. When the food enters your mouth, a juice, called the saliva, softens and wets it. Then your teeth cut and grind the food into smaller pieces and mix it with the saliva. This makes it easier to swallow.

After you swallow the food travels down a food tube, called the esophagus, and into a bag of muscle called the stomach. Here it is squeezed and churned and mixed with other juices to soften it.

When the food has become soft and thin, the stomach pushes it, a little at a time, into another long food tube. This is called the small intestine. Here the food is mashed some more and pushed along as it is mixed with still more juices.

By this time, the food has become thin and watery. The juices have changed or digested much of it in such a way that your body can use the goodness in the food. In the walls of the small intestine are many thin tubes with blood flowing through them. The food soaks into these tubes and is carried away in the blood to all parts of your body to give them the food they need.

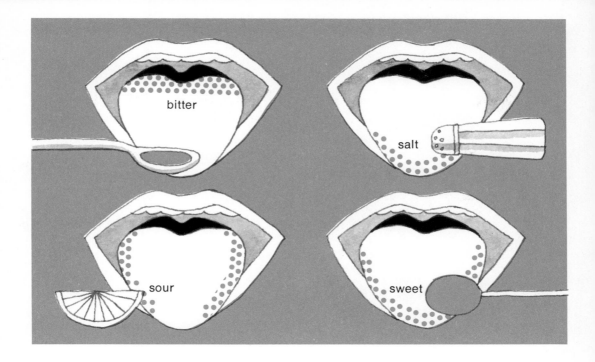

Why doesn't food taste as good when I have a cold?

When you bite into a chocolate bar, what do you notice first? The taste or the smell of the chocolate? The taste buds in your tongue tell you if something is sweet, salty, sour, or bitter. The smelling organs in your nose tell you if it is chocolate or gingerbread you are smelling. Taste and smell work together. When you have a cold, your nose is stuffed, and you cannot smell as well so foods do not taste as good.

Does my body use all the food I eat?

Usually your body uses most of the food you eat. When you eat too much, your body saves this food. It stores the extra food in special places, such as in layers of fat under your skin. Then when you need extra energy, such as in running a race, your body rushes this food to your muscles.

If you eat too much, too often, however, too much fat may be stored in your body. This is not healthy, and will also keep you from being slim and trim.

There are some parts of the food you eat that your body cannot use. Your body cannot use the woody parts of fruits or vegetables or too much water. These are called waste materials and move on from the small intestine into a larger tube called the large intestine and pass out of your body when you go to the toilet.

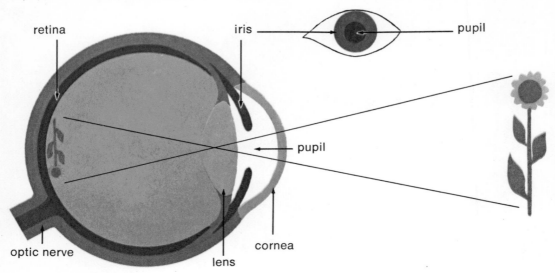

How do I see?

You can see colors. You can see big things, little things, square, pointed, and round things. You can see a plane high up in the sky and a tiny ant on the ground. You can see if something is standing still or moving. You see with your eyes.

In the front of each eye is a transparent covering, the cornea. Behind this is the colored part of your eye, the iris. In the center of the iris is a round hole called the pupil.

Light passes through the cornea and into the pupil. In bright light, the iris muscles partially close the pupil hole and make it smaller so too much light cannot go in and hurt your eye. In dim light, the iris muscles make the pupil open wider so more light can go in and you can see better.

Behind the iris is the curved lens of the eye. When the light enters your eye, the lens throws an upside-down picture on the retina, the lining at the back of your eyeball. The retina has millions of tiny cells that are connected to the optic nerve. The optic nerve sends a message to your brain and you see the picture right side up.

What color is the picture? Your eyes tell you that, too. In your eyes are nerves called rods. They re-act only to white. In your eyes are also other special nerves called cones. They alone can see red, blue, green, and other colors.

You see with your eyes!

Why do some people wear glasses?

Eyeglasses have special lenses to help a person see better.

Some people can see faraway things, but things nearby look blurred to them. They are far-sighted. Their eyeballs are a little too short. They wear glasses that help them see near things clearly.

Other people can see near things, but faraway things look blurred to them. Their eyeballs are a little too long. They wear glasses that help them see far things clearly.

There are many different kinds of glasses for the many different kinds of eye problems.

What do eyebrows and eye-lashes do?

They protect your eyes. Eyebrows keep sweat from trickling down into your eyes. Eyelashes help keep dust out of your eyes. They also help to shade your eyes from strong light.

What does my skin do?

Close your eyes and touch something. Was it hot or cold? Was it smooth or furry? Was it wet or dry? How do you know?

You know because you touched it, and nerve endings in your skin sent a message to tell you. That is one way your skin helps you.

Your skin helps in other ways, too. It covers your body and helps protect the inside part of you. It also helps your body keep at the right temperature.

Your body is always burning food to make heat. When you get too hot, you sweat. Sweat, or perspiration, is mostly water. As this water evaporates, your skin gets cooler. In your skin are many little tubes called sweat glands. They take water and waste out of your blood and push them out through tiny openings, or pores, in your skin. The air dries away the sweat, and you feel cooler. When you are in a hot sun or work or play hard, your sweat glands work harder so you sweat more than usual.

Your skin also has many other little tubes called oil glands. These glands send out oil to the surface of your skin to keep it soft and smooth.

Your skin helps you in many ways. You can help keep your skin healthy by keeping it clean!

Why do I shiver?

An icy winter wind is blowing, the frost nips your nose, and you are so cold that you shiver. Why do you shiver? Your body is trying to help you get warm. A shiver is a quick movement of your muscles. When you shiver, the muscle cells burn more food than usual to make more heat in your body. Then you feel warmer.

Sometimes it is fun to shiver. Do you like to listen to spooky ghost stories on Halloween? Do you pretend to be scared? You may shiver then, just for fun, but your muscles act in the same way as if you were very cold.

How does a cut heal?

If you cut your finger, the tiny blood vessels in your skin bleed. This helps wash away dirt and germs.

Soon your finger stops bleeding because the blood thickens, or clots. The thickened blood fills the cut. The blood clot hardens, little by little, until a hard scab is formed over the cut.

The scab covers the hurt place and helps keep germs from getting in. This is why you should not pick at the scab. Under the scab, inside the cut, new cells are building to fill the cut with new skin. The cut heals from the bottom up. When it is completely filled in, the scab falls off.

19

What are freckles?

In the summertime, do you get a deep, even tan or do you freckle? Or maybe you have freckles all year round! What are freckles?

In your skin are cells that make a dark coloring matter called pigment. When you are out under a hot sun, these cells work harder. If the cells are distributed evenly over your body, you get a smooth, even tan. But if the cells collect in small areas—such as on your face, neck, or hands—you get small brownish spots, or freckles. Some people freckle only in the hot sun. Others are born with freckles.

Why do people have differently colored skins?

We all have cells in our skin that make the coloring matter called pigment. But some people have only a little pigment and they have very fair skins. Others have more pigment, and their skins are darker. Your skin color depends upon how much pigment you have. And that usually depends on how much pigment your parents have. You inherit skin color from your parents.

How does my hair grow?

Each hair on your head grows from a tiny root. You cannot see this root for it lies deep down under your skin in a tiny tube called a follicle. At the bottom of each follicle are very small blood vessels that bring food to the cells. As the new cells grow, they push the old cells up into the follicle. Then the old cells change into hair.

Do you know that you may have about 60,000 hairs on your head?

Why do some people have curly hair?

Is your hair straight or a little wavy? Is it so curly that it is hard to comb? Whether your hair grows out straight or curly depends on the shape of your hair roots.

If your hair roots are round, your hair will grow out straight. If your hair roots are flatter, your hair will grow out curly. But whether your hair is straight, wavy, or curly, it will be beautiful if you keep it clean and brush it every day.

Why do some people have red hair and some brown?

The color of your hair, like the color of your skin, depends upon how much pigment you have. The skin cells that make pigment are deep in your scalp. It is the pigment that colors your hair blonde, red, brown, or black.

Why doesn't it hurt when my hair or nails are cut?
The only living cells in a hair, a fingernail, or a toenail are at the roots in your skin. There are no nerves in your hair or nails. So when they are cut, you feel no pain.

If your hair catches in a comb and you pull it hard, it may bring tears of pain to your eyes. That is because you pulled at the roots in your skin. A tiny muscle and nerve at the root of each hair sent a nerve message to your brain that it hurt!

If you stub your toe or break a fingernail, that too will hurt because you have hurt the skin under the toenail or fingernail.

What are fingernails and toenails for?
The nails keep you from hurting the soft tips of your fingers and toes. They are there to protect your finger tips and toe tips. Fingernails are also useful tools. Did you ever try to pick up a pin with very short fingernails?

Why do I sneeze?
You sneeze to get rid of something that doesn't belong in your nose. As you breathe in through your nose, the tiny hairs inside catch dust and germs from the air. But sometimes a little dust or dirt may get past these hairs. Then nerves inside the nose make you sneeze to blow away the dust or dirt.

You sneeze, too, when you have a cold. Such sneezes send germs into the air. To keep the germs from spreading to other people, always hold a handkerchief over your mouth when you sneeze.

How do I know how high to reach?

When you walk up or down the stairs you know how high to raise or lower your feet even if you don't look. When you reach for a light switch in the dark, your muscle sense, working with your sense of touch, tells you if your hand is at the right height. Close your eyes and try to draw a picture. How good was your picture? How good is your muscle sense?

What is muscle sense? There are special nerve centers in your muscles, tendons, and joints. They give you your muscle sense. They tell you how high to reach when you catch a ball or climb a tree.

Did you ever play pin-the-tail-on-the-donkey? When you play, you are blindfolded and you have to pin the tail on the cardboard donkey without being able to see it. Your muscle sense helps you do it.

Your muscle sense also helps you know how heavy a book or a beach ball or another object is and to use just the right amount of strength to pick it up.

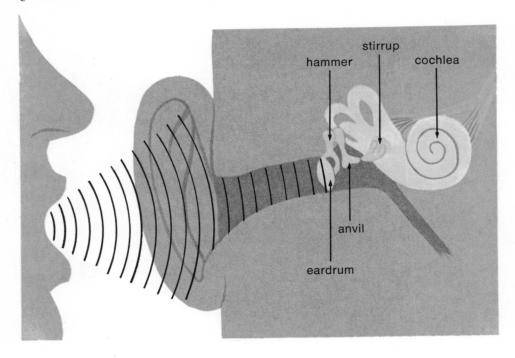

How do I hear?

You can hear rain pattering against the window. You can hear your mother calling you to dinner and your friend whispering a secret. You can hear the fire engine's siren and a car honking for you to get out of the way. You can hear soft sounds, loud sounds, many kinds of sounds. How do you hear?

You hear with your ears. You can see your ears, but it is the part of the ear you cannot see, the inside part of the ear, that makes you hear.

Listen to your kitten purr. The purr sets up sound waves in the air. The sound waves go into your ear and down a tube to your eardrum, a thin piece of skin stretched across the tube. The eardrum quivers, or vibrates, when the sound waves strike it. Three tiny bones, called the hammer, the anvil, and the stirrup, move with each vibration and carry the sound to a long tube that is curled up like a snail shell. This tube is called the cochlea. It is filled with fluid and in it are thousands of tiny nerve cells. They send a message to the brain. The brain tells you what the sound means. All this happens much faster than you can read about it.

How do I talk?

When you pluck the strings of a guitar, what happens? Try it and see. The strings move back and forth quickly, or vibrate. The vibrations make music.

You have a musical instrument or "voice box" in your throat. It is called the larynx. Inside the larynx, at either side, are tissue bands called vocal cords. When you talk or sing, air passes between your vocal cords and makes them vibrate. This produces sound much like the guitar strings produce sound when they vibrate.

Put your fingers on your throat and make a deep sound. Can you feel your voice box quivering?

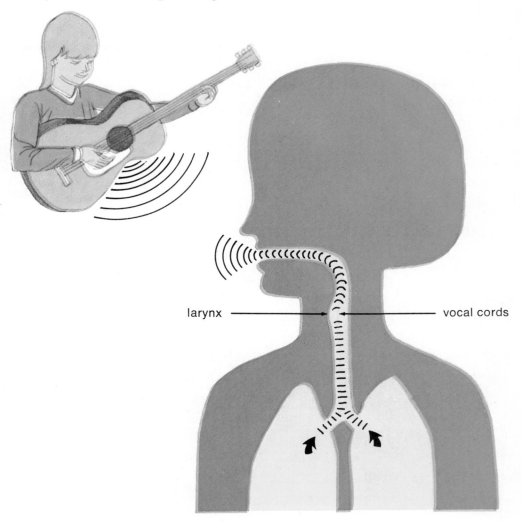

larynx ———————→   ←——————— vocal cords

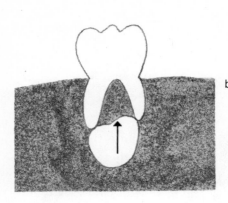
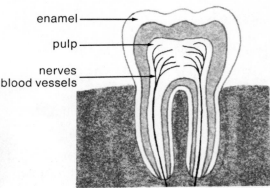

enamel

pulp

nerves
blood vessels

Why do my baby teeth fall out?

Your baby teeth fall out, one at a time, because they are being pushed by new teeth growing under them. Even when you were very young, your second set of teeth were already growing under your baby teeth. Did you know that you have twenty baby teeth? You have thirty-two teeth in your second set of teeth.

You should take care of your baby teeth until they fall out by themselves. The baby teeth protect your second set of teeth until these are ready to come out.

Why do I have to brush my teeth?

After all your second teeth grow out, no more teeth will grow in your mouth, so you must take care to keep them clean and healthy.

Your teeth are covered by a very hard material called enamel. Inside the enamel covering is a soft part called the pulp. In the pulp are nerves and blood vessels.

After you chew your food, often small bits of food stick between your teeth. Germs, called bacteria, that live on these tiny bits of food make the food rot. This makes a juice that eats into the hard enamel of your teeth and can make a hole, or cavity, in a tooth. The bacteria can also go into the soft inside of your tooth and harm it and give you a toothache.

A dentist can fill a tooth cavity, so you should see your dentist regularly. But you can help take care of your teeth and help keep cavities from forming. Brush your teeth after each meal, if you can. If you can't brush your teeth after you eat, then wash your mouth with water, especially after you eat sweet food.

26

How do I stand?

Birds fly, fish swim, kittens pad on four paws. But you can stand! Your skeleton is the reason why.

Your skeleton is made up of many bones and joints. Your bones work with your muscles to hold your body erect and help you run and jump.

You have many kinds of bones and each kind of bone is made in a special way to do a special job. All the bones work together.

You can't see your bones unless a picture called an X-ray is taken of them. But touch your finger. How many bones can you feel in it? Are they big or little?

The bones help you stand tall. They also help protect the inner parts of your body. They store minerals for use by cells in other parts of your body.

Do you know that you have more than two hundred bones in your body? You can help them grow strong and straight by standing erect and not slouching. Eating the right food, fresh air, exercise, and rest will help, too.

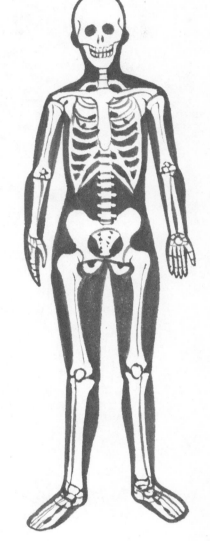

27

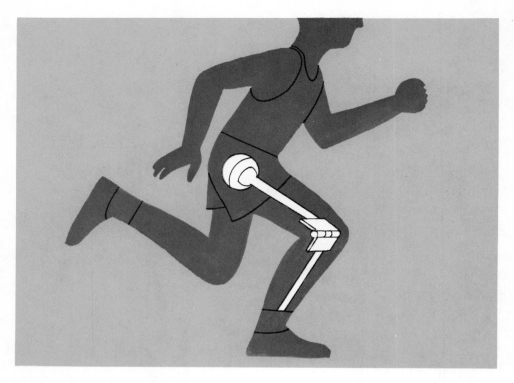

How do my bones join together?

The place where your bones fit together is called a joint. You have different kinds of joints in your body.

There is a ball and socket joint in your shoulder and hip. That is why your arm and leg can move freely in many directions. When you kick a football or throw a pass, you are using your ball and socket joint.

You have a joint that acts like a hinge in your elbow, knee, fingers, toes, and lower jaw. A hinge joint lets the bones move outward and back. Pick up a pencil. Could you pick it up as easily if your fingers did not bend? Say "Hello!" Could you say it if you could not move your jaw?

Why can I run and jump?

Your muscles help your bones move. They help you run and jump. You have more than five hundred muscles in your body. Do you know why you need so many? Stand up and walk. You just used about three hundred muscles!

The main job of your muscles is to help your bones move. But muscles also help keep your bones in their proper position and your joints firm. They help protect the inside of your body. When you shiver, your muscles are helping to warm your body.

Why do I need blood?

Blood is made up of millions and millions of tiny red and white cells floating in a liquid called plasma. The red blood cells carry oxygen, a gas found in the air, to every living cell in your body. Without oxygen you cannot live. The white blood cells, often called soldiers of the body, fight germs and help keep you well.

The plasma transports food to all the living cells in your body and carries away wastes, such as a gas called carbon dioxide. Blood moves in great circles from your heart to the cells and back to your heart again. Each round trip takes less than a minute. Without blood, you cannot live.

Everyone's blood is made up of blood cells, but the type of blood cells may be different. You and your best friend may have different types of blood. But although there are different types of blood, many different kinds of people have the same blood type. A red-haired girl and a blond boy may have the same type. A blonde boy and a dark-skinned boy may have the same type.

Why is blood red?

Blood is red because there are many more red blood cells than there are white cells. The red cells get their color from a chemical substance they contain. This substance is called hemoglobin.

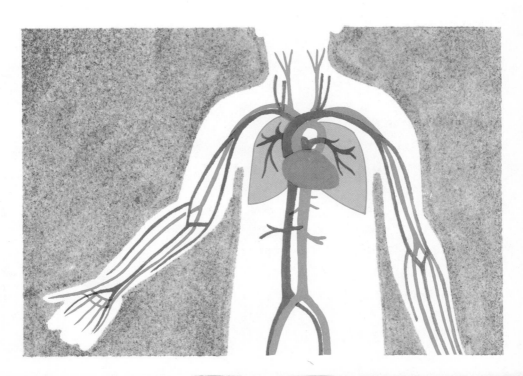

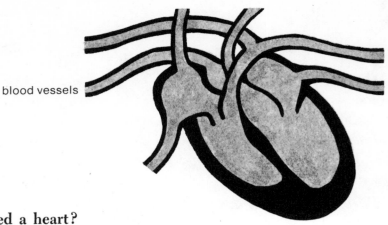

blood vessels

Why do I need a heart?

Your heart keeps your blood moving through your body—up to your head, down to your toes, and out to your finger tips. The blood moves through little tubes called blood vessels. Some of the larger blood vessels are as thick as your finger. They branch out into many smaller blood vessels, some thinner than a hair. Blood is always moving through these blood vessels even when you sleep.

Your heart is about the size of your fist. It does not look like a valentine heart. It is about the shape of your fist, too. It is made of strong muscles that pump the blood through the blood vessels to all parts of your body. If you put your hand over your heart, you can feel it beat.

Does my heart ever sleep?

Your heart never sleeps. Even when you are sleeping, your heart must keep pumping away to keep the blood moving through your body. Your cells need the blood so they can live and grow.

But, like your other muscles, your heart needs rest, too. It does rest for just a fraction of time after every beat.

Do I breathe when I sleep?

You start breathing when you are born and you keep on breathing all your life. You breathe when you are awake and you breathe when you are asleep. When you breathe in, you take oxygen from the air. Without oxygen, you could not live. When you breathe out, a gas called carbon dioxide goes out of your lungs.

While you breathe all the time, sometimes you breathe faster than others. When you are playing hard, you breathe fast. When you are asleep, you breathe more slowly.

What are nerves?

Your nerves are like tiny telephone wires that carry messages to all parts of your body. If you stick your toes into very hot bath water, you do not have to think what to do. Faster than you can think, the nerves in your toes flash a message, "Too hot!" to the spinal cord that runs through your backbone, or spine. From the spinal cord, other nerves flash a message back to your foot muscles, "Pull out fast!"

Nerves in your toes also send a message to your brain, "Too hot!" to let you know what is happening.

Nerves also send messages to your brain so you can know what you are touching, smelling, tasting, hearing, and seeing.

How do I think and remember?

Your brain helps you to think and remember and walk and talk and laugh and cry. Your brain controls your breathing and the beating of your heart.

Your brain receives and answers the messages from the nerves in all parts of your body. It keeps you alive.

Dogs, cats, and other animals have brains, too, but their brains are not like yours. The human brain is the most wonderful thing in the world.

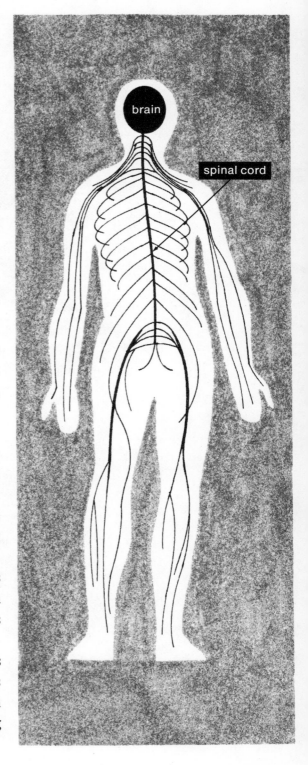

31

Children Ask
About Everyday Life

When I walk down my street, I wonder

—why are traffic lights green and red? How do they know when to go on and off?

—why do people live in different kinds of houses? I live in a house with a yard. Dan lives in an apartment house. Is it fun?

—why does Juan say "Buenos días" and Mimi say "Bonjour" when I say "Good morning"? Why doesn't everybody speak the same language?

—why does Johnny's mother go to work? Why doesn't she stay home as my mother does?

—if I lived in a faraway country, would I still know how to jump rope or play hide-and-seek or ball? Do children everywhere play the same games?

—how does the postman know where to bring my valentines?

—who can be President? Could I be President?

—I wonder if I could!

Why should I say "Please" and "Thank you"?

Why do you like some boys and girls and not like others? Is it the way they look? Or is it the way they act? How do you act to help people know you are friendly and polite?

"Please" and "Thank you" are little ways of showing friendly feelings toward people. When people hear you say these words, they know you have good manners, and that you are thoughtful and polite. Then they are glad to be friendly and helpful to you.

Of course just saying "Please" and "Thank you" is not enough. You want your friends to *be* thoughtful and considerate, and that is how they want you to be, too.

All around the world there are words for "Please" and "Thank you." In France, they say, "S'il vous plaît" and "Merci." In Spain, they say, "Por favor" and "Gracias." But if you say "Please" and "Thank you" to them and smile, they will understand and smile back. They will know you want to be friendly.

Who belongs to a family?

You and your mother and father are a family. Your brothers and sisters are part of your family, too.

Your mother's mother and your father's mother are your grandmothers. Your father's father and your mother's father are your grandfathers. They are part of your family, too.

Do you have aunts? They are your mother's or father's sisters.

Do you have uncles? They are your mother's or father's brothers.

Your cousins are the children of your uncles and aunts. And when your cousins have little boys and girls of their own, they will be your cousins, too. They are all part of your family, and you are part of their family.

Most families keep growing all the time. When did your family begin? Ask your grandmother to tell you a story about *her* mother. She was your great-grandmother!

Do you have a dog or cat? Are they part of your family, too?

Why are there different kinds of families?

Families are different in color, religion, and the way they live. Once, long ago, all the people who belonged to a family lived together. In some countries today, this is still true. But usually today only the father, mother, and children live together. The other members of a family live in homes of their own. Sometimes these homes are near to each other. Other times, they are far away.

Sue has three brothers and two sisters. Her grandmother lives in her house, too. Billy has no brothers or sisters. He is an only child. Meg lives with just her mother. Sue's family, Billy's family, and Meg's family are all different.

There are many kinds of families, and they live in many kinds of homes—big houses, little houses, apartments in a huge apartment building. They live in many different kinds of ways. But all families are alike in some ways. They need food, clothing, a place to live. Best of all, they are made up of people who belong to each other.

What is an adopted child?

Usually a child is born into a family, but sometimes he is chosen, or adopted. A mother and father do not have a baby, but they want one very much. They choose, or adopt, a baby to be their baby. Suppose Billy, who is an only child, wants a brother or sister. His parents, too, want very much to have another child. So they adopt one. An adopted child belongs to his family just as a child born into it does. His parents chose him to take care of and love.

Why do we need money?

Long ago there was no money. A family planted the corn or wheat they needed. The man hunted for deer for meat. The mother wove the cloth for their clothes. A man built his own house and the tables and chairs he needed.

Then people found that some farmers could raise better crops than others. Some people were better hunters or builders. So they began trading. A man would build a house and other men would pay him with wheat or wild deer. This was called barter. Today people use money to pay for things they need. When you go into a store and buy candy or a toy, you give money to pay for the goods and work that went into making that candy or toy. You are trading your money for that candy or toy.

Why do some mothers go to work?

Mothers work in different ways. Many mothers stay home and clean house, cook, and bake. Others go to work in stores, offices, and other places.

Meg and her mother are a family. Meg's mother works in a flower shop to take care of them.

Sue belongs to a big family. Her father works hard to take care of them all. At Christmastime, Sue's mother works in a store so there will be more money for Christmas presents.

Tom's father is a doctor. Tom's mother is a doctor, too. She works because she wants to help sick people get well.

What is a neighbor?

All the people that live around you are your neighbors. They live in your neighborhood.

Being a good neighbor means more than just living near other people. It means being friendly, helpful, and kind. It means doing the things that make other people feel friendly toward you.

We can be good neighbors to the people who live in our neighborhood and in other neighborhoods. We can be good neighbors to people who live a long way from where we live. We can be good neighbors to people who live in other countries.

How does a letter get to the right place?

When you send a valentine to your friend Beth, you put her name and address on it. The address is the number of her house, the name of the street, city, and state where she lives. You should also add the Zip Code so the post office can get it to her easily and quickly. This is what her address looks like.

> Miss Beth Adams
> 721 Elm Street
> Chicago, Illinois 60611

You also put a stamp on the envelope to pay the post office for delivering a valentine or letter to her.

Why do I have to go to school?

What do you want to be when you grow up? Do you want to fly a plane or be an astronaut? Do you want to be a doctor or a fire fighter? Do you want to be a nurse or work in an office or be a librarian? No matter what you want to be, you need to go to school to learn the things that will help you be what you want to be.

School also helps you learn the things you need to know right now. Do you like to play baseball or soccer? How could you keep score, if you did not know how to count? You learn how to count and use numbers in school.

Just for fun, for one day write down all the things you do. In how many of them do you need to use things you learned in school?

To begin with—you could not write, if you had not learned how to write. You could not read this, if you had not learned how to read! How many other things can you add to your list?

Who pays for the schools?

It costs money to build schools and have good teachers. The money comes from taxes. Taxes are paid by people to the government. Schools are so important that people pay school taxes even if they have no children. Taxes make it possible for us to have free public schools.

All children have to go to school, but they do not have to go to public schools. Instead, their parents can pay money, called tuition, to have them go to a private school. The most common type of private school is run by a church and is called a parochial school.

Why do we need policemen?

Policemen protect us by seeing that people obey the laws. Watch the policeman at your corner. Did you see him give a ticket to a man who was driving his car too fast? That driver could have hurt himself or someone else. The ticket orders the man to go to court, where he will have to pay a fine for disobeying the law.

There are many kinds of policemen. There are policewomen, too. They are all working to help keep us safe. Who tells the policemen and policewomen what to do? The police chief gives the orders for the police department.

Are you a patrol boy at school? Then you are a kind of policeman, too. You are helping protect the children as they cross the street.

Who pays the policemen?

Your father and mother help pay the policemen with the taxes they pay to your town or city. They know that the policemen work hard to try to protect us all. They know that policemen often risk their lives to protect us. The next time you see a policeman, remember he is working hard to help take care of you. Do you know a policeman? Ask him to tell you about his job!

Why are traffic lights green or red?

Next time it is dark and rainy, look at the traffic lights and see how they shine. Scientists say that red and green can be seen more clearly than other colors. That is why traffic lights are green for Go and red for Stop!

How do the lights know when to change? They are run by electricity and set to stay on for a certain time. They go on and off all day and night.

When you are crossing the street, be sure to stop and look to see what the traffic lights say. Be sure, too, to look both ways when you cross a street. Obey the safety rules and keep safe!

How does a fireman know which house is on fire?

Most fires are reported by phone. The person making the call tells the fire station where the fire is. Some fires are reported through a fire alarm box on a corner. A person breaks the glass on the box and pulls a little lever inside it. This rings the bell in the nearest fire station. It also lights up a number which tells the firemen where the fire is.

The firemen, too, work to help keep us safe.

Who makes the laws?

When you play baseball, you follow the rules. Three strikes means you are out. Your family has rules, too. Do you have to go straight home from school before you go out to play? That is a rule. When people live and work and play together, we need rules to follow so we will know what to do and to make sure that we are all treated fairly. A town, a city, a state, a country needs rules, too. We call these rules, laws.

Who makes the laws? Your father and mother make the rules for your family. But who makes the laws for a town, a city, a state, a country? There are so many people in our country that we cannot meet together in one place to make laws. That is why we choose, or elect, people to make the laws for us. We try to elect men and women who will make laws that are good and fair for all the people. Since we, the people, elect these lawmakers, we can say that in our country, we, the people, make the laws.

What is the government?

The people who make our laws are the government and are elected by all the people. Our government sees that we have firemen, police-men, parks, schools, hospitals, libraries and all the other things we need in our towns, states, and country. A mayor is usually at the head of a town or city. A governor heads a state government. The President is at the head of the government of the whole United States. The United States government is made up of three groups of men and women. One group makes our laws. A second group sees that the laws are obeyed. A third group decides if the laws are fair and settles any questions about the laws.

What is a citizen?

> *I pledge allegiance to the flag of the United States*
> *of America, and to the Republic, for which it stands,*
> *one nation under God, indivisible, with liberty*
> *and justice for all.*

When you say the *Pledge of Allegiance* in school, do you think of what you are saying? You are promising to be true to your country and to help make it the best country in the world for all its people.

A citizen is a person who belongs to a country and pledges allegiance to it. That means he will try to protect it, to obey its laws, and to help it in every way he can. When a citizen is old enough, he has the right to vote for the people who will make the laws, and he will try to vote wisely so that the laws will be good ones for all the people.

How do you become a citizen? If you were born in the United States, you are a citizen of the United States. If you were born in another country and come here and want to become a citizen, you must learn about our government and promise to help, not harm, our country. Then you can become a citizen.

A good citizen serves his country. And his country helps and protects him wherever he is, wherever he may go.

You are not old enough to vote, but you can be a good citizen now by doing what is right at home, at school, in your neighborhood, and in your city.

How is a mayor elected?

Election time is coming! It is time to elect a new mayor. John Jones wants to be mayor. Tom Smith wants to be mayor, too. Each has told the people why he thinks he could be a good mayor and make the town or city a better place to live in. The people have listened to them at meetings and watched them on television programs. They have read about them in the newspapers. They have decided which one they think would be the best mayor.

On election day, voting places open in each neighborhood. These places are open for only certain hours. The citizens who live in the neighborhood and who are old enough to vote can go there to choose the mayor they want.

Some voting places use sheets of paper called ballots. On the ballots are the names of John Jones and Tom Smith. Other voting places have voting machines. The names of John Jones and Tom Smith are on the machines, too.

To vote, a citizen goes into a small enclosed booth. He marks his paper ballot with an X before the name of the person he wants for mayor. If it is a voting machine place, he pulls a lever to vote for John Jones or Tom Smith. Nobody can see how he votes.

After all the votes are in, they are counted. The person who receives the most votes is the new mayor. The people choose the mayor they want to lead their city. They choose the governor of their state in the same way.

Who can be President?

Every four years, the people of the United States choose a President. The President leads the country. He has one of the hardest and most important jobs in the world.

Could you be President some day? The President must be a citizen who was born in the United States and who has lived here for at least fourteen years. He must be at least thirty-five years old.

Do you notice one thing? The President does not have to be a man. Maybe one day we will have a woman President!

Where are the American Indians?

Long ago, before the first white men came, the American Indians lived all over the land. They hunted or fished or built their villages where they pleased.

As more and more white men came, the Indians were forced off more and more of their land. The people in our government saw we had been unfair to the Indians, so they set aside, or reserved, land as reservations where the Indians could live. Today Indians do not have to live on reservations, but many still choose to do so. Many other Indians live wherever they choose to live.

Why do people speak different languages?

Do you have a little brother? Do you remember how he learned to talk? He learned from you and your family. When he was a baby, and you said "water," he tried to say it, too. If you speak English, he learned to speak English. If you speak Spanish or Japanese or another language, that is what he learned to speak. Babies learn to speak the language they hear.

Long, long ago, people lived in small groups. All the people in a group spoke the same language. As they began meeting other small groups and trading with them, they began to learn new words. Much like your baby brother, they learned to speak the words they heard.

If a group traveled south, for example, it began to use some of the words the southern people spoke. If it traveled north, it used some of the words of the northern people. Slowly the small groups grew big and became countries. Each country had its own language.

Today there are many languages spoken all over the world. But languages are still changing as new ideas and inventions arise.

Could I learn another language?

If you want to and are willing to try to learn another language, you can! You can learn in school or if you have a friend who speaks another language, you can learn from him. Why not try? It is fun and it will help you make new friends and understand them better.

46

Do children in all countries play the same games?

If we could travel together all around the world, what would we see? Boys and girls playing games! Would we know how to play the games they play? Some would be strange to us, but many would not.

In almost all countries, boys play ball. Sometimes the balls are big, sometimes they are small. Sometimes they are hard, other times they are not. Boys throw and catch balls, kick balls, hit them with a stick. The rules may be a little different than your rules, but you could play ball with them, too, and have fun.

Little girls play with dolls everywhere. Girls jump rope though the rhymes they sing as they jump are different in each country. Boys and girls play circle games.

Did you ever play, "Did you ever see a lassie
      Do this way and that?"

In France the children sing, "Sur le pont d'Avignon" as they play. In English the song goes like this:
      "On the bridge of Avignon,
      The boys bow this way."
You could play that game easily.

In almost all countries, children run races and play tag just as children have always done through the ages. Long ago in Rome, children played a kind of hopscotch. Long, long ago in Greece, girls jumped rope. Children in all countries play games!

Do different countries have different holidays?

Some holidays are celebrated in many countries around the world, although each country may have its own special way of doing so. How do you celebrate Christmas? Do you hang up your stockings and trim the Christmas tree?

In Mexico Christmas lasts nine days! For nine days before Christmas, Mexicans act out the story of Mary and Joseph searching for lodging, or posadas, before the Baby was born. Mexican children do not have a Christmas tree. They have a piñata. It is made of clay and often is shaped like a parrot or a donkey. The children form a circle. In turn, each child is blindfolded and given a chance to hit the piñata with a stick. When the lucky child breaks it, candy and fruit and small toys fall out.

In Holland, St. Nicholas comes on December 5th. He rides a white horse and the children set out their shoes with a carrot or bit of straw for the horse. If they are good, St. Nicholas puts presents in their shoes.

Christmas, Easter, New Year's Day are celebrated in many countries. But each country has some holidays that belong to it alone. In the United States we have the Fourth of July as our Independence Day. We have Thanksgiving Day, too. They are our special holidays.

How can I get to know children in other lands?

You can get to know children in other lands in different ways. Sometimes your father and mother may take you traveling to other lands, and then you can get to know them. But that is only one way.

You can get to know children in other lands while you stay home, too! Ask your teacher if your class can write to children in a school in France or Japan or Africa or any other country you all choose. Then you can get to know those children through their letters and they can get to know you through your letters!

You can read books about children in other lands, too. And someday, when you are older, maybe you will get a chance to travel to those lands and see them for yourself.

There is one more thing you can do. When children from other lands come to your town or neighborhood, you can make friends with them! They will be happy to have you welcome them, and you will find they have new and interesting things to tell you.

Why are some things easy to do and some things hard?

Danny is a good pitcher, but he strikes out almost every time he is at bat. Carl is no good at baseball, but he can build model planes. Sally can draw pictures that win prizes in the art show, but she has to study and study her spelling.

Danny and Carl and Sally are all different, just as you and your best friend are different. What things are easy for you to do? What things are hard? Almost everybody in the world finds some things easy to do and others difficult. Few people can do everything well.

We each have our own abilities or talents. That is what makes people interesting. Just think how it would be if everybody did the same thing in the same way!

Do you sometimes think that you do everything wrong? Everybody thinks that way sometimes. Just remember it isn't true. Think of all the things you *can* do. Maybe other boys and girls wish they could do them as easily as you do. And if there is something you want very much to do and that is hard for you, keep trying. Maybe you will be able to do it one day. Why not try and see?

Why must I stay away from strangers?
Do you like dogs? Most dogs are friendly. They bark and wag their tails to make friends. They like to have you scratch behind their ears. They like to play with you.

A few dogs are not friendly, and so you know that when you see a strange dog, you have to wait and see how he will act. Is he friendly, or will he snap at you?

You have to wait and see how strange people act, too.

Most people are friendly. They smile at you and you smile at them, and you make friends.

But a few people just pretend to be friendly. When you see a stranger near your playground or school or on your street, how can you know if he is really friendly? You have to wait and see.

Probably your mother and father have told you how to act to strangers, but here are a few rules to remember.

1 *Never go for a ride in an automobile with a strange man or woman.* Even if the stranger says that your mother or father says it is all right, don't do it. If your mother or father did say it, they will give him a note to tell you that.

2 *Never take candy or ice cream or anything else from a stranger.*

3 *If a stranger asks you to go anywhere, don't do it.* Tell your parents or teacher or any other grown-up you know who is near by.

People who are really friendly will never ask you to do anything your mother and father don't want you to do.

Children Ask
About Animals

I wonder

—why do birds fly away together when the weather gets cold? Can they talk to each other to say "Let's go now"?

—why does my cat hide her new kittens? I wouldn't hurt them.

—why do horses need shoes? Cats and dogs don't.

—how can a bear sleep all winter? Doesn't he get hungry or thirsty? How does he know when to wake up?

—how can a fly walk on the ceiling? Why doesn't he fall off?

—how can a duck sit in the water without getting her feathers wet? I get wet when I'm in the water.

—why do squirrels and birds and fishes have tails?

—how do fireflies make their tiny lights?

—why does a turtle live in a shell?

—*I wonder why!*

Why does a dog turn round and round before lying down?
Long, long ago all dogs were wild. They hunted for their own food
and slept in the tall grass. To make a soft bed, they turned round
and round and flattened the grass before lying down. Today most
dogs are tame, but they still turn round and round as they get ready
to lie down.

Do you know there are still some wild dogs today? A wild dog that
lives in Australia is called the dingo. Dingos are fierce and savage
and hunt together in packs. When the wild dingos howl, koala bears
and other small animals keep out of their way!

Can all dogs bark?
The wild dingo howls but does not bark. Another barkless dog is the
basenji that comes from Africa. It makes a yodeling sound when it is
happy and it growls when it is angry, but it cannot bark. The basenji
is a friendly dog and likes children.

Why does a dog pant?

When you are too warm, you sweat over most of your body. This makes you feel cooler. Your dog can sweat only through the bottoms of his paws. When he is hot, this is not enough to cool him, so he pants. As he breathes air in and out quickly, he gets rid of heat inside his body and feels cooler.

Where do little puppies come from?

Puppies grow inside the mother dog in somewhat the same way that peas grow in a pod. Each puppy is fastened to the mother inside by a little cord. Each one is in a little bag, or sac, that has a liquid in it. The liquid acts as a cushion to keep the puppy from being hurt. Puppies do not need to eat or breathe while they are inside the mother because they get food and air from her. When they are grown enough, the puppies are pushed out of the mother. The sac around each puppy breaks. Then the puppies can breathe. The mother licks her puppies clean. While they are young, puppies drink milk from the mother dog's nipples. This is their food.

Can dogs see colors?

Your dog can hear sounds you cannot hear. When he sniffs along a trail, he can smell scents you cannot smell. But if you throw a ball for him to fetch back to you, he will not know if the ball is green or red or yellow. Dogs cannot see colors. All things look white or black or gray to them.

How can a cat see in the dark?

If you put your cat in a room with no windows and closed the door tightly so no light came in, your cat could not see. But if you let the slightest streak of light come in, your cat could see. Look at your cat's eye in the daylight. Notice that the dark part in the center, the pupil, is closed to a narrow slit. This keeps the bright sunlight from hurting your cat's eyes.

In the dark, the pupil of your cat's eye opens very wide. This lets in a great deal of light. That is why your cat can see more at night than you can see.

Why does a mother cat hide her new-born kittens?

When kittens are born, they are tiny and helpless. Their eyes are delicate until they are fully open. The mother cat hides her kittens in a dark place to keep them safe and to keep the bright light from hurting their eyes.

Why are lions and tigers called big cats?

Lions, tigers, leopards, panthers, and your furry small kitten all belong to the same family, the cat family.

56

Is a pony a baby horse?

No, a baby horse is called a foal. A pony is a small horse that is less than 58 inches or 14.2 hands high. You measure a pony or horse in hands. A hand is 4 inches. You measure a pony from the ground to the ridge between his shoulder bones, or his withers. Some ponies, like the Shetland pony from Scotland, are no bigger than a large St. Bernard dog. It is fun to ride a pony, and he can live happily on just good grass in summer, good hay in winter, and plenty of exercise.

Why do horses need shoes?

A horse's hoof is really a very large, thick toenail. When horses ran wild on pastures, they did not need shoes. But when a horse must carry people or pull a load over hard ground, rocky trails, or city streets, his hoofs may get chipped, cracked, or worn down. So he wears horseshoes to protect them. Your dog and cat do not need shoes. They do not carry people on their backs.

Why do people look at a horse's teeth?

If you know enough about horses, you can tell a horse's age by his teeth. A horse's teeth change as he grows older. By the time he is six months old, he has all his baby teeth. When he is about three years old, these teeth begin to fall out and new ones begin to grow. At five years of age, he should have all his second teeth. As the horse grows older, his teeth wear down and become shorter. Do you see how you can tell a horse's age by his teeth?

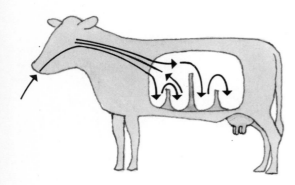

Why does a cow chew a cud?

Why does a cow keep chewing and chewing when it isn't eating? A cow belongs to a group of animals called ruminants.

When a cow eats grass, she does not take time to chew it well. The grass is only moistened before it is swallowed and passed on to the first part of the cow's stomach. This first part is called the rumen. In the rumen, the grass is collected, mixed, and softened and passed on to the second part of the cow's stomach. There the food is formed into little balls, or cuds. Later, while the cow is resting, the cuds are returned to the cow's mouth and chewed again. This second chewing is called "chewing the cud."

After this chewing is finished, the cow swallows the food again and it goes to the third part of the cow's stomach where the moisture is squeezed out. Finally it goes to the fourth part of the cow's stomach where it is digested.

Goats, sheep, deer, camels, and giraffes chew cuds, too. They are also ruminants.

Do other animals give us milk?

A cow gives us milk. Some people also drink the milk of reindeer, goats, and camels.

How can a bear sleep all winter?

When it gets very cold, most bears crawl into their dens to sleep until warm weather comes. They eat a great deal of food in the summer and fall and this food is stored in their bodies as fat. They live upon this stored fat while they sleep away the cold weather. On warm days they awaken, eat more food, and then go back to sleep.

The sleeping bear is said to be dormant. Some animals, such as woodchucks, lizards, snakes, frogs, and turtles, sleep without waking until spring. They are said to be hibernating.

Why do skunks have a strong smell?

If you see a furry black animal with broad white stripes along the sides of its back, take care not to frighten it or make it angry!

A skunk moves slowly and it defends itself from enemies by spraying a very bad-smelling oily fluid that is stored in two scent glands inside its body near the base of the tail. If it hits the eyes, the liquid can cause temporary blindness. The bad smell lasts a long time and is almost impossible to remove from clothing.

Why does a kangaroo carry its baby in its pocket?

When a baby kangaroo is born, it is very tiny and has no hair or fur on its body. The little kangaroo needs to be kept warm and safe. Its mother's pocket, or pouch, is snug and warm. Inside the pouch there are nipples which give milk to the baby when it is hungry. The baby kangaroo lives there until it is big enough to hop around by itself. Kangaroos live in Australia.

Why does a gorilla beat its chest?

A gorilla lives in central Africa. It is a huge ape and may be six feet tall and weigh about 400 pounds. A gorilla beats its chest to frighten its enemies, and it looks and sounds so wild that other animals and most people usually run away!

What is an elephant's trunk?

Some elephants live in Africa and others live in India or on islands in the Indian ocean. An elephant is a surprising animal. It is the biggest of the land animals, but it does not eat meat. One of the most surprising things about an elephant is its trunk. Its trunk is both its nose and its upper lip and may be seven feet long!

An elephant can do many things with its trunk and is very careful of it. With its trunk, it can gather food from the ground or a branch of a tree. It can squirt dust or water over its back. It can blow water into its mouth. It can sniff the air and catch the scent of another animal as it comes near.

What is a dinosaur?

Millions of years ago, animals called dinosaurs roamed the earth. Dinosaur means terrible lizard.

There were many kinds of dinosaurs. Some were small, but many were huge. Brontosaurus was a huge dinosaur who lived in a swamp. He was about seventy feet long, but he ate only plants.

Tyrannosaurus rex was another huge dinosaur. He stood about twenty feet high and was about fifty feet long. He ate meat and was probably the fiercest animal that ever stalked the earth.

Stegosaurus was huge, too. He was about eighteen feet long and had great bony plates, like armor, along his back.

Some dinosaurs had horns.

Triceratops had three horns and he, too, had bony armor.

Pteranodon was a huge flying dinosaur. His wings spread out twenty-five feet!

While dinosaurs were different in many ways, they all had small brains. They all had lungs to breathe air and they laid their eggs on land.

Dinosaurs disappeared long ago, but scientists have found their eggs, bones, and footprints buried in earth. These have told them much about life in ancient times.

What is the largest animal?

The largest animal known to have lived on land or in the sea is the blue whale. It is much bigger than an elephant. One blue whale was measured at 106 feet.

Is a whale a fish?

Whales live in the water and are shaped like fish, but they are not fish. Whales belong to a group of animals called mammals because they give birth to their babies and feed them milk. Most baby fish are hatched from eggs the mother fish lays.

Whales breathe with lungs as you do, but fish breathe with gills. Whales are warm-blooded while fish are cold-blooded.

Why does a whale spout?

When its lungs are full of used air, a whale comes up to the surface of the ocean to get fresh air. The warm, wet breath is forced out through one or two blow-holes in the top of the whale's head. The stream of warm, wet air sometimes forms a little cloud if the weather is very cold. This happens to you, too, when you breathe out on a cold day. Sometimes, too, the whale blows before its head quite reaches the top of the water. Then a spout of water shoots up with the air as it blows out.

blue whale

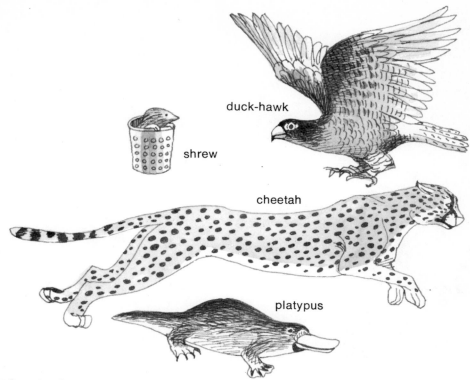

duck-hawk

shrew

cheetah

platypus

What is the smallest animal?

The smallest animal is so tiny that you cannot see it without a microscope. It is an animal with only one cell and belongs to a group of animals called protozoans. Usually they live in the sea or still water ponds.

The smallest mammal is the shrew. Some full-grown shrews are so small they can fit into a thimble. One of these tiny shrews may weigh less than a penny.

What is the fastest animal?

The hunting leopard, or cheetah, can run the fastest. Some cheetahs can run as fast as seventy miles an hour. But the fastest animal of all is a bird called the duck-hawk. When it chases a duck, it may fly at a speed of over 160 miles an hour.

What is the strangest animal?

The strangest animal lives in Australia. It is called the duckbilled platypus. It has fur and feeds its babies milk, so it is a mammal. But it lays eggs like a bird and has webbed feet and a bill like a duck's. Its tail is like a beaver's tail. It is timid and shy, but if you watch a river or lake in eastern Australia, you may see one.

What animal lives the longest?

A big land turtle, called the tortoise, may live to be over 125 years old. An elephant may live for seventy years. A crocodile and a rhinoceros may live to be fifty. And the eagle, the parrot, and the swan may live almost as long.

Why do animals need tails?

Did you ever watch a horse or a cow switch its tail to brush away the flies? Then you know how tails help them. The tail feathers on a bird help it steer through the air currents as it flies. A beaver spanks the ground or water with his broad, flat tail to tell other beavers that danger is near. A squirrel uses his tail as a rudder to balance as he leaps through the trees. A kangaroo leans on his tail to help himself stand up. A fish uses its tail as it swims. And what would your dog do if he couldn't wag his tail to tell you how glad he is to see you?

Do animals talk to each other?

When you watch birds flying south together in the autumn sky, do you wonder how they all meet together? Do they tell each other when they are going? We do not know that, but scientists do know that birds talk to each other in a way. A robin and a song sparrow have different songs, but each has a call that says "Danger! Look out!" Each kind of bird has a mating call, a hungry cry, a call that says, "Stay away. This is my tree. I'm building my nest here."

A cow moos, a horse whinnies, a lion roars. The sounds they make are different, but each makes a happy sound, an angry sound, a danger sound, a hungry sound. Listen to a cat purring to her kittens or a dog barking at her puppies. Can you understand what they are saying? Can the kittens or the puppies understand?

How can you tell one animal track from another?
Look at the track a horse makes. Does it look like a rabbit's track? How is it different? If you see a track and do not know what animal made it, try to find out! Does the track show that the animal walked heavily? Did it run or hop? Did it drag its tail? Where does the track lead? If you follow the track, you may find out where the animal lives and what it eats. You may even find the animal! That is why you should be careful what animal track you follow.

Is a bat a bird?

A bat can fly, but it is not a bird. A bat has fur, but a bird has feathers. A bat has sharp teeth, while a bird has no teeth. A baby bat is born and gets milk from its mother. A baby bird is hatched from an egg. Like other animals that give birth to their babies and feed them milk, a bat is a mammal. It is the only mammal that flies. Like many birds, however, a grown-up bat eats insects.

How can a bat fly in the dark without bumping into things?

A bat can fly in the darkest night without bumping into walls, trees, or other things around it. How can it do this? As a bat flies, it gives a high-pitched squeak that people cannot hear. The squeak makes small waves of sound in the air. When the sound waves hit a tree or wall, an echo bounces back. A bat's hearing is so keen that it can catch that tiny echo and dodge out of the way of that tree or wall.

Is a bird an animal?

Every living thing is either a plant or an animal. Most animals can move, although they may move in different ways. A bird can move. It hops and flies. Animals get their food by eating plants or other animals. A bird eats seeds and insects.

A bird is an animal. It belongs to the large group of animals called vertebrates, animals with backbones. Kittens, fish, frogs, and snakes are some of the many other vertebrates. They all have backbones although their backbones are shaped in different ways. You have a backbone, too!

How can a bird fly?

Next time you see a bird in the air, watch its wings. See how they beat up and down, always moving! They are pushing the bird through the air.

The air is forced to move faster over the curved top part of the wings, but it pushes up at the bottom of the wings. This lifts the bird in the air. The wing and tail feathers help the bird steer through the air, too.

A bird's body is shaped so it can move easily through the air. Most of its bones are hollow and filled with air, so a bird does not weigh much for its size.

There are birds of many sizes and colors. The shapes of their wings vary, too, according to their needs. A hummingbird does not fly like an eagle, but whenever a bird flies, its wings are always moving in the air.

penguin   ostrich

Can all birds fly?

Some birds have wings, but cannot fly. Among these are the ostrich, the kiwi, and the penguin.

The ostrich is the largest living bird. Its wings are too weak to lift its heavy body. It runs swiftly across African grasslands on its long, strong legs, and its wings help it balance as it turns.

The little kiwi of New Zealand has very short wings and no tail. It hides in the forest during the day and comes out at night.

The penguin has wings like flippers. It uses them as paddles when it dives and swims under water.

Where do birds go in the winter?

In winter, many birds fly south to a warmer climate. In the springtime, they come back. We call this migration. Why do birds migrate? When cold weather comes, it is hard for some birds to find food. Perhaps they fly south because food is plentiful there. We do not know exactly why birds migrate, but scientists are trying to find out. One way they do this is by banding birds.

The band has a number on it. It is fastened on the bird's leg and a record is made showing the date, place, kind of bird, and the band number. Then the bird is let loose to fly away. If that bird is caught again, the scientist can tell where it flew and how long it took the bird to get there.

The champion bird traveler is the Arctic tern. It may fly 22,000 miles in one year. Many terns make their nests and raise their families near the North Pole. As soon as the young terns are old enough, all the birds fly south to the Antarctic, near the South Pole. These birds fly over open water and live on fish as they travel.

What is the largest bird?

The ostrich is the largest living bird. It may grow to be eight feet high and weigh about 345 pounds. But it cannot fly. Probably the largest flying bird is the Wandering Albatross. It lives in the southern oceans and its outspread wings measure about ten feet from tip to tip.

What is the smallest bird?

The tiny hummingbird is so small that when it gathers nectar from a flower, people often mistake it for a moth. One kind, the ruby-throated hummingbird, is only about two and one-half inches long.

Can a bird fly backward?

The hummingbird can fly backward and straight up. When a hummingbird hovers over a flower, it looks as though it were standing still in the air. Its wings beat so fast you can hardly see them move!

Why do birds have different kinds of bills?

The hummingbird's long, slender bill can reach deep into a flower to get nectar and insects. Its bill is just right for the kind of food it eats.

A pelican eats fish. He needs another kind of bill. His bill is just right for catching fish. And under his bill, he has a pocket, or pouch, where he can keep the fish until he eats them.

Birds have different kinds of bills to help them get the food they need. That is why a duck and an eagle, a sparrow and a woodpecker, all have different kinds of bills.

hummingbird

eagle

wood-
pecker

pelicans

How does a duck keep its feathers dry in the water?

Ducks have soft, fluffy feathers, called down, that are so thick and fine that water cannot get through them easily. Over the down is a covering of heavier feathers. At the base of a duck's tail is a special oil gland. With his bill, a duck takes this oil and spreads it over his feathers. This is called preening. The water cannot soak through this oil and the duck is waterproof!

How does a hen make eggs?

Each egg starts from a tiny egg cell inside the hen. As the egg grows larger and larger, it moves down a tube. When the egg is large enough, the hen forces it out. At first the egg shell is quite soft, but the air hardens it quickly. For a time, a hen may lay an egg a day. It takes a number of days for the egg to grow. So the hen has several eggs growing inside her body at one time.

Did you ever see a hen sitting on her eggs? She is hatching them, keeping them warm so baby chicks can grow inside them. It takes about three weeks for the eggs to hatch. In the yellow part of the egg is a tiny speck. As this speck grows, it uses the yellow yolk for food. The speck grows and grows until it almost fills the shell. It is no longer a speck but a little chick with a bill, eyes, legs, wings, and feet. When it is ready, it pecks open the shell, and breaks out. A baby chick is born!

How can a snake travel without legs?

A snake really moves by making its skin crawl. The horny scales or plates on the snake's belly move as the snake bends its body from side to side. The rear edges of the scales grip the ground and keep the snake from slipping back. That is why a snake can move faster on rough ground than on a smooth surface.

Where do snakes keep their poison?

The two large teeth of a poisonous snake are hollow. The poison comes through each hollow tooth from a sac in the snake's upper jaw. The sacs make the poison and hold it until the snake squeezes it out through the tips of his teeth, or fangs. Sometimes these fangs are more than half an inch long.

Why does a turtle live in a shell?

The turtle's shell is really part of its skeleton. Some turtles have shells that are rounded. Others have shells that are flat. The shell is a bony box that protects a turtle from its enemies. When a water turtle gets into the water, it can paddle around or zoom down into the water like a submarine, shell and all. Some turtles can pull in their head, neck, legs, and tail and close the shell tight when danger threatens.

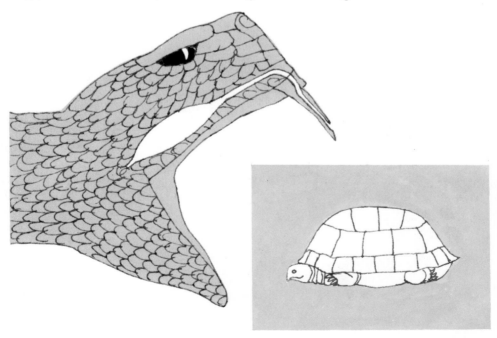

Are tadpoles fish?

Tadpoles are not fish. They are frog babies. After a mother frog lays her eggs in the water, they hatch into tadpoles. When a tadpole is first hatched, it has no eyes, legs, or mouth. It does have a tail and a sucker. Soon the tadpole begins to swim by flipping its tail. It grows gills so it can breathe. Its mouth and eyes grow.

During the next weeks, lungs develop and the gills disappear. Now the tadpole has to swim to the top of the water to breathe. Its legs grow and its tail grows shorter and shorter until it is all gone. Then the tadpole is no longer a tadpole. It is a frog!

Toad babies are tadpoles, too, and grow in much the same way. When an animal lives the first part of its life in water and then lives on land, we say it is an amphibian. Frogs and toads are amphibians.

Are fish animals?

Fish are animals with backbones, or vertebrates. They have gills so they can breathe in water. Some fish, like the tuna, live in the oceans. Others, like the golden trout and carp, live in freshwater lakes or rivers.

Some fish are pets. Do you like to watch goldfish swim in a bowl?

Why don't fish drown?

You need oxygen to live. You get it from the air when you breathe. Fish need oxygen, too, but they get it from water.

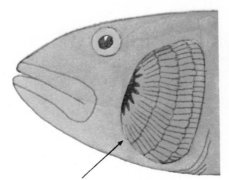

A fish has gills to breathe with. When a fish breathes, the gill covers on each side of its head open and close as water is taken into the fish's mouth. The water is not swallowed. When it passes back over the gills and out under the gill covers, the gills take oxygen from it.

gill (cutaway sketch)

Do fish sleep?

Fish have no eyelids, so they cannot close their eyes. But they do rest quietly at the bottom of the water. Watch goldfish in a bowl. Can you see them resting?

How can fish live when a pond or lake freezes?

A pond or small lake may freeze so that there is a covering of solid ice for you to skate on, but usually under that ice is water. The water that flows into the pond or lake brings fresh oxygen for the fish in it to breathe. Usually, too, there are air holes at the edges of the pond that also let in oxygen.

If the pond were frozen from top to bottom, there would be no oxygen. The fish would die.

What is a sea horse?

A sea horse is not a horse, but a tiny fish, seldom more than six inches long. It lives in the ocean. Its head with its long snout looks like a horse's head at first glance. Like other fish, it breathes oxygen from the water through gills. It has little eyes, but cannot see far. Its body is covered with bony rings or plates.

A sea horse swims slowly with its head straight up. The sea horse is unusual in another way. The mother sea horse lays her eggs in the father sea horse's pocket, or pouch. He carries them around with him until they hatch. After they hatch, he still carries them in his pouch until they are grown enough to find their own food.

Does a fish feel pain when you hook it?

A fish has few nerves around its mouth, so it feels little pain when it is hooked.

Are there really flying fish?

There are fish that sail through the air. They leap out of the water and glide for a short distance on their large fins. They are called flying fish although they do not fly the way a bird does.

74

Does a bee die after stinging you?

When a bee stings you, the hooks in its stinger catch in your flesh. The bee cannot free the hooks so when it flies away, the stinger and part of its body are torn off. The hurt bee cannot live. A bee uses its stinger to protect itself and its hive.

A bee sting can be dangerous, so if you see a bee buzzing around, do not try to catch it. Usually if you let it alone, it will fly away. If you do get stung, try to scrape off the stinger right away so less of the poison will get in. If your eyes or lips swell or you feel very ill, call a doctor.

How does a bee hum?

When a bee beats its wings, it makes a humming sound. The wings move so fast, you cannot see them move.

How does a bee make honey?

A honeybee has a long beak and a hollow tongue. It climbs into a flower. With its tongue, it sucks up a sweet juice, nectar. The nectar is carried into the bee's special honey stomach. This is not the stomach it uses to digest its food. In the honey stomach, the nectar is mixed with special chemicals. When the bee returns to the hive, muscles squeeze the nectar back into the bee's mouth. The nectar is put in the honeycomb where it turns into honey.

What makes a firefly's light?

On a summer's night, little sparks of light flicker and glow under the trees. Did you ever try to catch a firefly and wonder what made its light? Scientists do not know exactly why a firefly lights up, but they do know how the light is made. There are two special chemicals in the body of a firefly. When these chemicals mix with oxygen in the air, they give off a cool light.

How do crickets sing?

Listen! Can you hear the crickets chirping? The sound you hear is the male crickets singing to the female crickets. Lady crickets do not sing. The male cricket makes its music by rubbing its wings, one over the other. One wing has a row of ridges. The other wing has a hard little scraper. When one wing rubs over the other, we hear a cricket chirp or sing.

How can a fly walk on the ceiling?

Why doesn't a fly fall down when it walks on the ceiling? Flies have pads on the bottoms of their six feet. A sticky substance on the pads holds the flies to the ceiling.

How can a caterpillar turn into a butterfly?

When you look at a caterpillar crawling on a leaf and watch a butterfly soaring in the air, do you know that a caterpillar hatches out of a butterfly's egg?

At first the caterpillar is tiny, but it eats and eats and as it eats and moves about, it grows and grows until it is too big for its skin. Then a wonderful thing happens. The skin splits and comes off, and underneath is a new skin. This is called molting. The caterpillar eats and grows and molts until it is fully grown. Then it stops eating and crawls under a twig. There it spins a pad of silk and fastens itself to the pad. Hanging from the twig with its head down, the caterpillar sheds its skin for the last time. This time, the skin underneath hardens into a chrysalis. Now the caterpillar is in its resting, or pupa, stage.

Inside the chrysalis, the caterpillar is changing. Its body turns into a creamy liquid. Four wings, six legs, new eyes, and feelers, or antennae, form. Then one day, the chrysalis splits open. Out crawls a butterfly with wet, folded wings. The butterfly waits until its wings unfold and dry. Then it flies away!

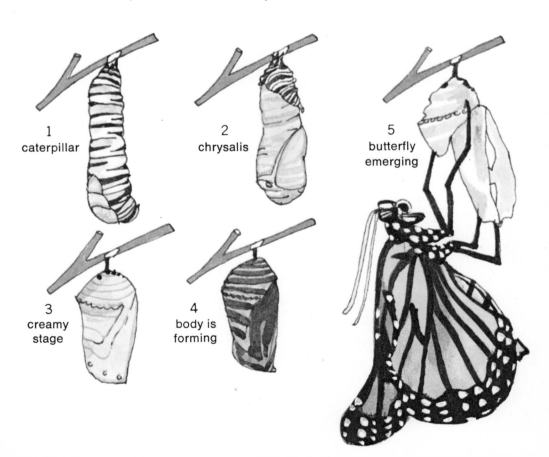

1
caterpillar

2
chrysalis

5
butterfly
emerging

3
creamy
stage

4
body is
forming

How does a spider weave its web?

A spider weaves its web from a kind of liquid silk that is made inside its body. As the silk is drawn outside, it hardens into a thread. At the hind part of her body, a spider has three pairs of spinners, or spinnerets. These spinnerets weave the threads into thicker strands. Some of the threads are dry, others are sticky.

Different kinds of spiders weave different kinds of webs. A garden spider weaves a web that looks like a wheel with spokes. Other spiders weave webs that are shaped like funnels. But no matter what pattern a spider uses, her web is beautifully made. The webs are made to trap insects which the spider eats.

How can a spider walk on its web without getting tangled in it?

When an insect flies into a spider's web, it is caught in the sticky threads and cannot get loose. Can the spider walk on its web without getting caught, too? A spider is careful to walk only on the dry threads in its web. But even if it slips and touches the sticky threads, it is not caught because its body has an oily covering that protects it.

Will an earthworm die if it is cut in two?

It depends on where the earthworm is cut. If just the tip of the worm's head is cut off, it may grow a new tip. If the tail is cut off, the worm may grow a new tail. But if the earthworm is cut in two even parts, it will die.

How does a worm get into an apple?

The worm does not get into the apple. It is born there! A small fly picks the apple as the place to lay her eggs.

The fly has a sharp, hollow tube on her underside. With it, she pokes a hole in an apple. Then she lets her eggs slide down the tube into the apple. When the eggs hatch, they are little worms.

The worms eat tunnels into the apples. This is their food. When the apple falls to the ground, the worms crawl out and burrow into the ground. A hard, outside skin forms around each worm.

All winter the worms stay in the ground. Inside their hard skins, their bodies are changing into flies. When summer comes, they come out of their skins, and they fly away.

What is a starfish?

The starfish is not a fish, and it is not a star. It is an animal with a spiny skin and arms that look like a star. The sea star has five arms. The sun star has many more arms. A starfish lives in the ocean and has gills to breathe with. It also takes in oxygen and gives off carbon dioxide from the walls of its tube feet.

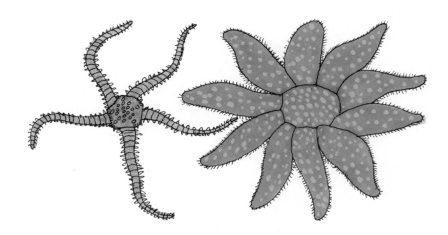

Children Ask
About Plants

I wonder

—why does a morning-glory close in the afternoon? Why does a four-o'clock open then? Can flowers tell time?

—why do leaves turn red and gold in the autumn? Pine needles don't.

—why don't trees die in the winter?

—how do wild flowers get planted?

—why do bees fly to flowers?

—how can you tell how old a tree is?

—how can you tell one tree from another tree?

—how do plants eat? Do some plants really catch insects? Do they eat them?

—were there always trees and flowers? What is the oldest plant in the world?

—*I wonder!*

How are plants and animals alike and different?

Watch a squirrel scamper up a tree. Can you tell how the squirrel and the tree are alike? The tree and the squirrel are both alive. They grow. A baseball bat cannot grow bigger. A doll cannot grow. Living things can grow. Plants and animals are living things.

Plants need food to grow. They need air, water, and some warmth. Animals need all these, too.

Plants and animals are alike in another way. A mother squirrel has baby squirrels. A robin hatches eggs from which baby robins may grow. An apple tree has seeds from which other apple trees may grow. Only living things can produce living things like themselves.

How are plants and animals different? Most animals can move. Most plants cannot move.

There is another important difference. Green plants make their own food. Animals cannot do this. They must get their food from green plants or from other animals that eat green plants.

How do plants make their own foods?

Green plants make their own food from air, water, minerals, and light. Each green leaf has tiny openings, or pores. When we breathe, we take in oxygen from the air. Through its tiny pores, a green leaf takes in a gas, called carbon dioxide, from the air.

A green plant needs water, too. Water enters a plant through its roots and comes up through the stems. The water carries minerals from the soil into the plant.

Do you know why leaves are green? In the cells of a green plant is a green substance called chlorophyll. It colors the leaves green.

Chlorophyll does an even more wonderful thing. When light shines on a green plant, the chlorophyll changes the water and carbon dioxide into sugar. This is an important part of the plant's food. Then most plants change part of the sugar into another kind of food before they store it away. A potato plant changes much of its sugar into starch and stores it in its underground stem. A pea plant forms protein from its sugar and stores it in its seeds.

The way green plants make their own food is called photosynthesis. This means making something with the help of light.

The foods green plants make for themselves also provide food for us to eat. Peas, for example, provide some of the proteins we need.

Why do we need plants?

If there were no plants, there would be no animals on earth. There would be no cows, for cows eat grass. There would be no chickens, for chickens eat grain. There would be no birds, for birds eat grain and insects that eat grass. There would be no fish, for big fish eat little fish that eat tiny water plants. There would be no lions or tigers, for lions and tigers eat animals that eat grass.

What would you eat? There would be no milk, for milk comes from a cow. There would be no eggs, for eggs come from a chicken. There would be no hamburgers. Everything you eat—except salt and water—comes from plants or from animals.

Plants give us our food. They give us many other things, too. Plants give us wood, paper, and rubber. They give us cotton and linen. Coal was formed from forests that grew millions of years ago. Oil was formed from tiny plants and animals that lived in shallow seas long, long ago. Look at this picture. How many things can you see that were made from plants or from animals that eat plants?

Why do leaves change color in autumn?

When autumn comes, the leaves turn red and gold and orange. Where does the green go? What paints the leaves with bright colors?

In the spring and summer, the trees are growing. Their leaves are green with chlorophyll that helps them make food to grow. By autumn the trees have stored enough food to keep them alive during winter. A cork-like ring of cells grows between the leaves and their twigs. These cells keep water from flowing into the leaves. Without water, the leaves cannot make food, and the green chlorophyll disappears. Now the bright colors that were always in the leaves blaze forth. Other chemical changes also take place in the leaves to make them burn red, gold, scarlet, orange, yellow.

Why don't trees die in winter?

In the winter, the twigs and branches of many trees are bare. You can see cork-like scars that show where the leaves grew. A tree takes water from the ground through its roots. In cold weather, the ground freezes. No water enters the tree. The tree must keep the water it already has, or it will dry up. The corky scars on the twigs and branches help seal the water in the tree.

The tree's sap thickens and goes deep in the tree. The sap holds the food the tree has stored. The tree lives on this food during the winter. The tree's bark is like a blanket that covers the tree and keeps the sap from freezing. In the bark are tiny openings, or pores, through which the tree breathes in winter. All winter the tree rests. In spring, the sap rises. New leaves grow and begin to make food.

Why do pine trees keep their needles in winter?

The leaves, or needles, of a pine tree have thick outside coats and few openings, or pores. The thick coat and shape of the needles help keep the pine trees from losing too much water and from freezing so pines do not need to shed their leaves in winter. Some needles may stay on a pine tree for years. Pine trees, hemlocks, cedars, and other fir trees are called evergreens because their needles are always green. Even when their needles change, you hardly notice because a new needle grows before the old needle falls.

What is bark?

Bark is the skin of a tree. If you peel off a little bark, you will see a wet, light-colored layer underneath. This is the living part of the tree's trunk. New bark keeps forming here, but the outer layers of the bark are dead. The dead layers protect the living part of the tree from drying and freezing. They also protect it from insects and other enemies that might harm it. If you make a cut in the bark, new cells will grow to cover the cut. But be careful not to cut too deep.

How can you tell how old a tree is?

The living part of a tree is just under the bark. Each spring this part grows fast. It forms a light-colored layer of wood all around the trunk. As the growing season advances, new wood is formed more slowly and is darker. When a tree is cut, you can see these rings in the wood. If you count the rings, you can tell how old the tree is.

How can you tell trees apart?

A pine has needles. A maple and oak have leaves. How are their leaves and shapes different? A tree's shape, bark, and leaves will help you tell trees apart.

oak

pine

maple

How do plants breathe?

We breathe with our lungs. When we breathe in, we take a gas called oxygen from the air. When we breathe out, we return a gas called carbon dioxide to the air. Plants take in carbon dioxide through the tiny openings, or pores, in their leaves. They need carbon dioxide to help make their food. When they let out air through the tiny pores, they return oxygen to the air. We need oxygen to breathe. That is one way we and plants help each other.

Do plants sleep?

Plants do not sleep as we sleep, but they do rest. Many trees rest in winter. The bulb of the iris plant rests in winter, too, while its flowers and leaves die. In the spring, new flowers and leaves grow from the iris bulb.

Most plants rest during cold weather, but many plants also rest at their own special times. The morning-glory opens its flowers early in the morning, and closes around noon. The four-o'clock gets its name because its flowers open around four in the afternoon. The evening primrose doesn't open until the sun goes down!

Can flowers tell time? No. If there is no sun, the four-o'clock will not open at four o'clock. It responds to the sunlight.

The dandelion is even more particular. It doesn't like wet weather. On a rainy day, its flowers are closed. When do the flowers in your garden open and close?

Why do plants have flowers?

Morning-glories are pretty to see, but plants do not have flowers just to please us. The gay color and fragrance of the flower attracts a bee, and this will help the morning-glory make new seeds. Plants have flowers so they can make seeds.

If you look at a flower bud that is ready to burst open, you will see that it is covered by tightly overlapping little leaves, or sepals. When the flower opens, the sepals spread apart and the petals unfold. Inside the flower are tiny stalks with knobby heads. These are the stamens. The tiny knobs are bags, or sacs, that hold a feathery powder called pollen. Most flowers have yellow pollen.

The pollen helps the flower make seeds. A violet can make seeds from its own pollen, but most flowers cannot. The pollen must be carried from one flower to another flower like it. The wind carries the pollen from some flowers, but many flowers depend upon bees, butterflies, or moths to carry their pollen.

When a bee sucks the sweet juice, or nectar, from a morning-glory, some of the flower pollen is brushed off onto the bee. Then the bee flies to another morning-glory and some of the pollen shakes off into the new flower and helps it make seeds.

What does a bee get from a flower?

When a bee sucks nectar from a flower, it is getting food. It also brushes some of the flower pollen into tiny pollen baskets on its hind legs. It carries the nectar and pollen to its hive. There the bees make honey from the nectar and bee bread from the pollen.

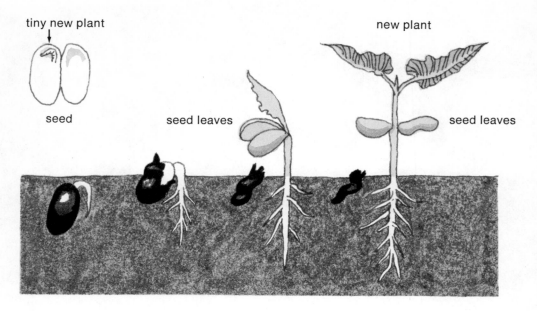

tiny new plant

seed

seed leaves

new plant

seed leaves

How does a seed turn into a plant?

If you split open a lima bean, you can see a tiny new plant in it. At one end of the stem are two tiny pale leaves folded tightly together. When the seeds become warm and wet enough, the little stem sends a root down into the ground. The root soaks up water. The little plant grows. As it gets larger, it splits the seed cover. The stem grows longer. Leaves come out and unfold. The two halves of the seed are also fastened to the stem-like leaves and are called seed leaves. The baby plant gets food from them. Before this food is used up, the true leaves turn green and begin to make food.

How do plants spread?

Did you ever plant an apple tree? If you ate an apple and threw away the seeds, maybe you did! Birds and other animals also help plants spread. A robin carries away a cherry in its beak. It eats the cherry and drops the seed. A cherry tree may grow. A squirrel carries away a nut which is the seed of a nut tree. It buries the nut and a new nut tree may grow. Bees and butterflies carry pollen from one flower to another and so help plants spread.

The wind helps many plants spread. A maple tree has seeds with tiny wings. When the wind blows, the seeds fly away. When we plant seeds, we help plants spread.

Do all plants have seeds?

If you take a walk in the deep woods where it is shady and moist, you may see leafy green ferns growing. Ferns have no flowers or seeds. On the bottom of a fern leaf are small brown dots. These are really little cases and in each case are many tiny spores. The spores are so tiny you can see them only with a microscope. When the spore cases are ripe, they pop open and throw the spores in the air. The wind blows the spores here and there. If they land on soil that is damp and moist and where there is not too much sun, the spores live and grow.

Mushrooms grow in the woods, too. Like ferns, mushrooms have no seeds. They, too, have spores. Mushroom spores grow best in warm, moist soil. Most mushroom spores need shady places to grow.

Other plants reproduce in different ways. Yeast plants grow tiny bumps that become new yeast plants. Bacteria plants are one-celled plants. They reproduce by dividing in two.

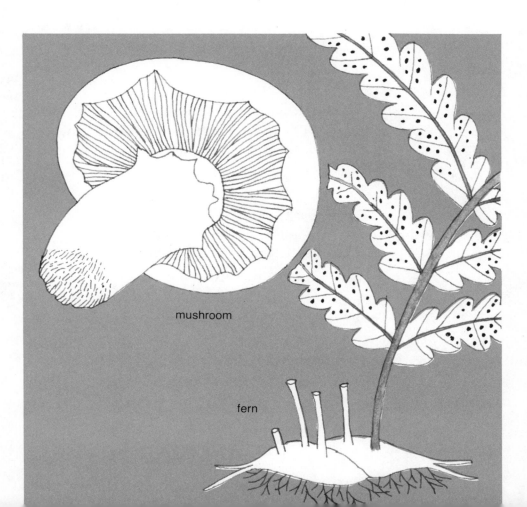

mushroom

fern

How can plants live in water?

Many plants live in lakes, rivers, ponds, and the ocean. Some are tiny. Others are huge. Like other plants, they need carbon dioxide to breathe. Land plants take the gas called carbon dioxide from the air. Water plants take it from the water.

Some seaweeds are green. Others are red, blue, or brown, but they all have the green substance called chlorophyll. This helps them make their own food. To make food, they need sunlight. Sunlight reaches only a short way into water, so most water plants live in shallow waters or on the surface of deep waters. When the sun shines on the plants, the chlorophyll changes the water and carbon dioxide in them into food. We need water plants because they help make food for fishes and for other water animals.

Can desert plants live without water?

Cactus plants live on the desert and need very little water. Some live only during the rainy season. When the dry season comes, they die. When the rain falls again, their seeds sprout and grow.

Other cactus plants have special kinds of stems or leaves that help them hold the little water that falls on the desert. Cactus plants also have roots that grow near the surface of the earth. This helps them take in water quickly when it falls before it dries up.

Because they need little water, cactus plants are sometimes called camels of the plant world.

Do some plants really catch insects?

The pitcher plant, the sundew, and the Venus fly trap are plants that do catch insects. These plants often grow in soil that does not give them enough food-making materials.

The pitcher plant has leaves that look like tubes. Inside the tubes is a sweet, sticky juice. When insects crawl down to get the juice, tiny hairs on the inside of the tube-like leaves catch them and stop them from getting out. They fall to the bottom and are digested.

The sundew plant has sticky hairs on its leaves. When an insect lights on a leaf, it is caught and the hairs and leaf curl in and trap it.

The Venus fly trap has a leaf with a kind of hinge down the middle. The leaf has hairs on it, too. When an insect lights on the leaf, the sensitive hairs re-act and the two parts of the leaf close over the insect.

What is the oldest plant?

The first plants that grew millions of years ago were tiny and simple and lived in water. As the years went on, the plants grew larger. Some began to climb the rocks near them. They developed pores so they could take carbon dioxide from the air. Plants began to grow on land. Our plants today are not like those first plants, but ferns are relatives of ferns that lived long, long ago, although they are much smaller now.

sundew

pitcher plant

Venus fly trap

What is the smallest plant?

Bacteria are the smallest plants we know. They are so tiny you can see them only under a microscope. If you looked through a microscope at different kinds of bacteria, you would see that some are round, others are shaped like rods, and still others have curly shapes. Bacteria are one-celled plants. They make new plants by dividing in two. They divide and divide so quickly that they can make more plants like themselves faster than any other plant we know today.

What is the largest plant?

The largest plants that grow on land are trees. Some sequoia trees that grow in California are more than three hundred feet tall. Some measure more than thirty feet around their base. The giant sequoia is one of the oldest plants, too. One of them is believed to be more than 3,000 years old.

Another giant of the plant world is the redwood tree of California. Muir Woods, near San Francisco, is a national monument for the preservation of these trees.

The largest water plants are kelps, seaweeds that grow in the ocean. These plants may grow more than a hundred feet long. They, too, live for many years.

What are weeds?

Sometimes a weed is just a plant that is growing in the wrong place. If a stalk of corn grew in a field of wheat, the farmer would call the corn a weed because it did not belong among the wheat.

Some weeds are harmful. Poison ivy is a weed. If you touch it, blisters or a rash may form on your skin. Other weeds, such as the dandelion, do not harm human beings but are bad for other kinds of plants. They take the water and food from the soil that nearby desirable plants need. Often they grow taller than these plants and keep the sunlight from them. Most weeds also grow very quickly. Weeds are enemies of lawns, garden flowers, and crops.

How do scientists find out about plants and how they grow?

Scientists who study plants are called botanists. They study plants that grow today and plants that grew millions of years ago. When they find traces of ancient plant life in rocks, they try to find out what the plant looked like and how it grew and developed.

Scientists study living plants to find ways to make them grow taller or stronger, or to have prettier flowers, or to provide greater amounts of food for us to eat. They also try to find ways to protect plants from diseases and ways to prevent weeds from growing.

Children Ask
About the World
Around Us

I wonder

—how high is the sky? Could I ever touch it?

—why can't I see the wind? I can see things blowing. I can feel the wind tugging my hair. What makes the wind blow?

—why does my shadow keep changing? Sometimes it is long, sometimes it is very short, sometimes it isn't there at all.

—where does the sun go at night?

—why do the tides go in and out?

—why does the ocean taste salty?

—why do the waves change color? Sometimes they are blue, sometimes they are almost black.

—where do the rain puddles go after the sun comes out?

—if the earth is round, why don't we fall off?

—*I wonder why!*

What is air? How high does it go up?

Air is everywhere around us. We cannot see air, but when the wind blows, we can feel air. The wind is air in motion.

Air is made up mostly of two gases, nitrogen and oxygen. We need oxygen to breathe and live. Carbon dioxide is another gas in air. Green plants need carbon dioxide to make their own food. There is water in air, too. It makes clouds and fog, rain and snow.

The blanket of air around the earth is called the atmosphere. It goes up several hundred miles. Near the earth, the air is dense or thickly packed, because the air above it pushes down on it. Higher up, the air become thinner and lighter until there is no air at all. This is where space begins.

What makes a balloon go up?

A toy balloon filled with helium, a very light gas, will go up in the air. The reason is that helium is lighter than the air around it. When the balloon reaches air as light as helium, it stops going up.

What makes the wind blow?

The sun can make the wind blow! When the sun shines down, it warms the earth and the air around it. Warm air is lighter than cool air, so the warm air rises. Cooler air moves in to take its place. When the air moves slowly, there is a breeze. When the air moves fast, there may be a wind storm! The sun is always shining here or there. The air is always moving. The wind is moving air.

What makes a whirlwind?

Most whirlwinds happen over the desert. The sun beats down on the dry sands and the air near the land becomes very hot. It rises suddenly and whirls or spins. As it rises, it takes some sand and dust with it. This helps us see the whirling motion in the air.

What is a tornado?

A tornado is a whirling wind storm that blows very fast. It has a dark funnel-shaped cloud that spins quickly. It makes a great roaring sound. A tornado is not big, but it is the most dangerous of all winds. It blows so strongly and so fast that it can lift buildings and carry them away or smash them like toys. Often a tornado causes terrible destruction.

Why is the sky blue?

How blue the sky looks! Do you know that blue is only one of the colors in sunlight? All the colors of the rainbow are mixed together in sunlight. As the sun shines through the air, its light is broken up, scattered, and stopped. Only the blue light bounces away to reach us. It makes the sky look blue. If you zoomed high above the earth in a rocket, where there is no air to break up the sunlight, the sky would look black, not blue.

Why is the sky red at sunrise and sunset?

When the sun is low in the sky in the morning and evening, its light must pass through a thicker layer of the air around earth. Much of the color in sunlight is stopped, but the red light shines through.

What makes a rainbow?

Air breaks up and scatters the colors in sunlight. Raindrops can do this, too. When sunlight shines through raindrops in just the right way, the light breaks up into bands of violet, indigo, blue, green, yellow, orange, and red. We see a rainbow. You can make a rainbow if you choose. On a sunny day, turn on the sprinkler. Stand with your back to the sun. You will see a rainbow in the spray!

100

What makes colors?

An apple is red. But if you looked at an apple tree on a dark night, the apple would look dark. You would not see the red.

Light makes colors! All the colors are in sunlight. When the sun shines on a red apple, the apple reflects the red light in sunlight. It stops, or absorbs, all the other colors in sunlight. Where there is no light to reflect, the apple looks dark.

An object that reflects some color and absorbs other colors in light is called opaque. An apple is opaque. What color is window glass? No color! A window glass does not reflect or absorb color. Colors pass through it so we say that it is transparent.

We see colors with our eyes. In our eyes are nerves called rods. They re-act only to white. In our eyes, too, are other nerves called cones. They help us see colors. When light strikes a red apple, it reflects red light to the cones in our eyes. We see a red apple.

We can see colors. We can make colors, too. Did you ever mix colors with crayons or paints? Yellow and blue make green. Yellow and red make orange. What do red, yellow, and blue make?

What makes shadows?

Did you ever try to run away from your shadow? You can't do it! Do you know why? Light cannot shine through you. When light falls on you, your body stops or blocks off some of the light. The place that is blocked off from light is dark. You throw a shadow!

Sometimes your shadow is little. Sometimes it is huge and long. It depends on how the light falls on you. If the light comes from above you, your shadow is small. If the light strikes you from a lower angle, your shadow is longer. Stand in a dark place where there is no light. Can you see your shadow?

Why is it dangerous to look directly at the sun?

The sun is a ball of fiery gases. It is so hot that it shines with a burning light. The sun's rays can give you a sunburn. If you look directly up at the sun, it can also burn your eyes.

Where does the sun go at night?

The sun does not move. The earth turns itself around every twenty-four hours. The earth is always spinning from west to east. At sunrise our part of the earth is turning toward the sun. We have day. At sunset our part of the earth is turning away from the sun. The sky is dark. We have night.

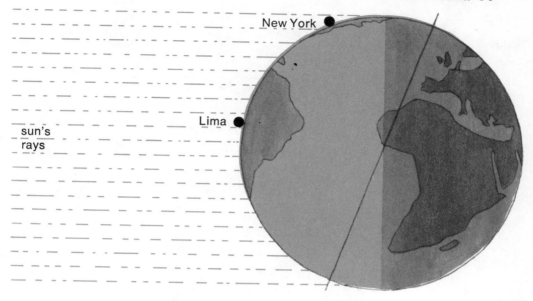

New York

Lima

sun's
rays

Why is it hot in summer and cold in winter?

The earth's axis is an imaginary line running through the North Pole
and the South Pole. As shown in the drawing, the axis is tilted in
relation to the sun's rays. The part of the earth tilted toward the
sun gets more of the sun's light and heat. It has summer. The part
of the earth tilted away from the sun gets less of the sun's rays and
it has winter. In the drawing, it is winter in New York and summer
in Lima (a city in South America) because the earth's tilt causes
Lima to be nearer to the sun than New York.

The earth is always moving around the sun. It takes the earth a
year to make a full turn. In six months, when the earth has made one-
half a turn, the tilt will cause the North Pole to be nearer to the sun
than the South Pole. It will be summer in New York and winter in
Lima.

If the earth is round, why don't we fall off?

Throw a ball up into the air. Does it stay up? No, it falls down. A
pull, or force, in the earth pulls the ball down. This force is called
gravity. The earth's gravity pulls everything toward the center of
the earth. It pulls on the land and the oceans and the air. It pulls on
everything on the earth. It holds us to the ground.

Why does water in a lake look blue?

Look down into a lake. Can you see your face in the water? Like a mirror, the water reflects your face. It reflects the color of the sky, too. When the sky is sunny and blue, the waters of lakes and oceans look blue. When the sky is cloudy and dark, the waters look gray and dark. When there are tiny green plants in the waters, the waters look green.

What makes the tide come in and go out?

Did you ever build a sand castle on the beach and watch the ocean waves creep up on the sand? With a surge, they roll over your castle. The tide is coming in, covering the sand. Later the tide will roll out again. The sand will be bare. You can build another castle.

At certain times each day, the tides come in and go out. What makes the tides? The moon moves about the earth as the earth moves around the sun. As the moon passes over an ocean, the moon's pull, or gravity, tugs at the waters. The earth's gravity pulls at the ocean waters, too, holding them to earth. The ocean waters rise and fall. When the waters rise, the tide comes in. When the waters fall, the tide goes out.

Why is the ocean salty?

For billions of years the chemical elements that make up salt have been washed out of the soil and rocks by falling rainwater. As these elements are carried to the ocean by rivers they combine to make salt. When the sun's heat makes some of the ocean water go up into the air, or evaporate, the salt stays in the ocean and the ocean gets saltier and saltier.

How deep is the ocean?

The deepest place we know in the ocean is near the Mariana islands in the Pacific ocean. The ocean is nearly seven miles deep there.

What is at the bottom of the ocean?

High mountains and deep valleys lie at the bottom of the ocean. Many strange animals and plants live there. Nickel, copper, and many other minerals are also found there. Scientists, called oceanographers, are now exploring the ocean deeps in submarines, diving saucers, and other underwater machines.

How do rivers begin?

Somewhere it rains, or perhaps snow melts. Not all the water sinks into the ground. Some water runs down to lower ground to form a little stream. Then many little streams run together to make small rivers. The small rivers pour their waters into big rivers. The big rivers flow into the oceans.

What makes floods?

When a heavy rainstorm or fast melting snow or ice pour too much water into a river too quickly, the river cannot carry the water away. The river fills to the top of its banks and water overflows onto the land. There is a flood. Often houses and trees are carried away. We help prevent floods when we plant trees and other plants. Water sinks into their roots. It does not run off as quickly into the river.

Why do people build dams?

A dam holds back water in a river. The stored water can be used by cities and towns, and also for crops. Dams help prevent floods by holding back the extra water and later releasing it slowly. At many dams, electricity is produced by using the stored water to turn huge generators inside the dam.

What makes clouds?

In the air there is a gas we cannot see, a gas called water vapor. When warm, moist air rises from the earth, the water vapor cools up in the sky. It turns into tiny droplets of water. These droplets join with tiny particles of dust to make clouds.

There are many kinds of clouds. On sunny days, big fluffy white clouds float in the blue sky. These are cumulus clouds. Delicate, feathery clouds high in a sunny sky are cirrus clouds. Dark, heavy clouds low in the sky are nimbus clouds, and it will probably rain!

What is fog?

Fog is really a cloud that lies close to the earth. Fog can be so thick and gray that you cannot see the house across the street. City fog is often thicker than country fog because there is more dust and soot in the city air to mix with the water vapor.

What makes rain?

When the water vapor in a cloud forms bigger and bigger drops, the cloud grows heavier and darker. When the drops are too heavy to stay up in the air, they fall as raindrops.

107

What makes lightning and thunder?

When Benjamin Franklin flew a kite in a thunderstorm about two hundred years ago, he discovered what lightning is. Lightning is a huge electric spark. Lightning sparks build up in clouds. Suddenly there is a flash! Lightning can jump from one cloud to another cloud. It can jump from a cloud to a tree or other object on earth.

When lightning flashes through the air, it heats the air quickly. The hot air pushes out. Cold air rushes into the empty space with a bump, a crash, a rumble! We hear thunder. Lightning causes thunder.

Why do we see lightning before we hear thunder?

You see a flash of lightning streaking across the sky. Then you hear the rumble of thunder. Light travels faster than anything else in the whole universe. It travels about 186,000 miles in just one second. Sound travels more slowly. It travels only one mile in five seconds.

Next time you see lightning, count the number of seconds before you hear the thunder. Divide the number by five. That will tell you how many miles away the lightning struck.

What makes windows get steamy?

Everywhere there is water in the air. You cannot see the water. It is in the form of an invisible gas called water vapor. When water vapor in the air of a warm room touches a cold window, the water vapor cools. It changes into tiny droplets of water that cling to the window. Soon there is a steamy place on the glass. If you put your finger on the steamy place, you can feel the wetness.

Blow on a cool window. Your warm breath will make a steamy place.

What makes windows get frosty?

When water vapor in the air of a warm room touches a cold window, it turns into tiny droplets of water. When it is very cold outside, the water droplets freeze into frost. Sometimes you can see flowers or stars in the frosty picture on the window glass.

What happens to puddles after rain?

You walk down a street or a country lane and there is a rain puddle. The sun shines down and soon the puddle is gone. Where did it go? The sun's heat made some of the water go up into the air, or evaporate. Some of the rain water also sank into the ground. If trees or grass were near, the water went into their roots to help them grow.

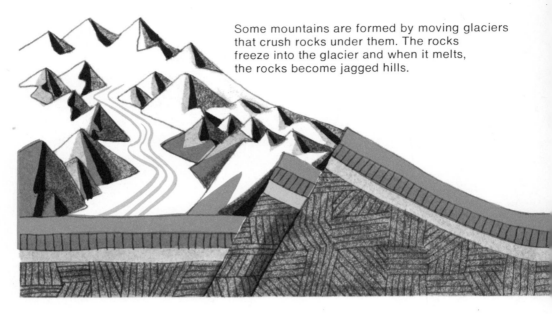

Some mountains are formed by moving glaciers that crush rocks under them. The rocks freeze into the glacier and when it melts, the rocks become jagged hills.

What makes sleet and hail?

Sleet and hail are frozen rain. Sometimes during a rainstorm, the blowing winds toss raindrops high up where the air is very cold. The raindrops freeze into ice. Some fall to earth in tiny icy needles, and we have sleet.

Some of the frozen raindrops may be caught by upward gusts of wind as they begin to fall. The wind tosses the icy drops back into the clouds. When they reach the warm parts of the clouds, the frozen drops get wet again. Again the wind blows them up into the high cold air and more ice forms on them. The frozen raindrops get bigger. This can happen again and again. The icy raindrops may get bigger and bigger until at last they are so heavy that they fall to the ground as hail. Some hailstones may be as big as marbles. Others may be much bigger.

What makes snow?

In winter the water vapor in clouds may turn into ice crystals instead of rain. The icy crystals fasten on to dust specks in the air. Then a crystal may join itself to another crystal. Many of these tiny icy crystals joined together make a snowflake. When the snowflakes are heavy enough, they fall from the clouds. We have snow. Each snowflake is different. No two snowflakes are ever alike.

110

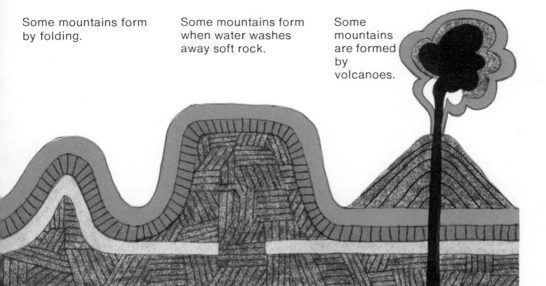

Some mountains form by folding.

Some mountains form when water washes away soft rock.

Some mountains are formed by volcanoes.

How are mountains made?

It takes millions of years to make a mountain, and mountains are made in different ways.

In some places on earth, hot gases blow hot liquid rock out of holes in the ground. The hot liquid rock is then called lava. The lava mixes with hot ashes that are also blown from the holes in the ground. Little cone-shaped hills form. The lava cools and hardens into rock. As more and more lava and ashes blow out, the hills grow higher and higher until they are mountains. These are called volcanic mountains. Some of the highest mountains in the world were formed in this way. Mount Aconcagua in South America is one of them.

Other mountains are formed when water washes away soft rock and leaves ridges or peaks of hard rock standing. That is the way the Catskill mountains in the state of New York were made.

Many mountains are made in still another way. Gravity is always pulling all the earth toward its center. The inside of the earth is also cooling and shrinking. As the inside shrinks, the outside crust of the earth must wrinkle, or fold, to fit into the smaller space. This outside crust is thick and hard. As it folds, it sometimes cracks or breaks. Some pieces of rocky crust are tilted upward. Other pieces overlap each other. Mountain ranges are usually made in this way. The Swiss Alps are one of these mountain ranges.

What is a volcano?

In some places under the hard rocky crust of earth there are pools of hot liquid rock, or magma. Magma moves around inside the earth. Sometimes it seeps out through a crack in the earth's crust. Other times it bursts out or erupts in an explosion. When the hot liquid rock escapes from the earth, it is called lava. The hole from which it erupts is a volcano.

The hot lava and volcanic ash that erupt from the earth form a cone-shaped hill. As they cool, they become rock. More and more lava and ashes are added to the hill and it builds into a mountain. Some volcanoes erupt on land. Others erupt at the bottom of the ocean. They build higher and higher until they are islands. The Hawaiian islands were made by volcanoes.

What makes earthquakes?

When the earth quakes and quivers and cracks, we have an earth-quake. The earth's crust is very hard but gravity is always pulling it toward the center of the earth. When the pressure is too strong, the rocky crust of the earth cracks. Volcanoes can also make earthquakes.

How do diamonds get into the ground?

If you went digging for a diamond in a mine, do you think you would know a diamond when you found it? It would not look sparkling and bright like a diamond ring. It would be in mineral ore. Ore is a rocky material. It must be treated in a special way to get the diamond out of it. Then the diamond must be cut and polished.

Most rocks are made of minerals. Some have only one mineral in them. Quartz is a rock like this. Glass is made from quartz.

Most rocks have several minerals in them. Granite has three. They are quartz, feldspar, and mica. Sometimes there is hornblende instead of mica in granite. If you find a speckled pebble, it may be granite. But not all granite pebbles look alike. Some have tiny chunks of minerals in them. Others have bigger chunks. The feldspar may be pink or light gray. The mica may be black or silver-white in color.

Diamonds and tourmalines and opals and other precious stones are made up of minerals, too. Like granite pebbles, two opals or diamonds or tourmalines or other jewels do not always have exactly the same colors.

diamond

tourmalines

opals

113

What is soil made of?

Do you remember the soft squishy feel of soil when you made mud pies? Do you like to dig for worms or plant roses or sweet corn? Next time you work in soil, look and see how many things you can find in it.

Soil is made from tiny pieces of rocks that come from the rocky crust of the earth. Heat, cold, ice, wind, water, and growing plants slowly wear away the rocks. They break the rocks into smaller and smaller pieces. The pieces of rock in soil are often so small you cannot see them. Sometimes you will find a pebble or two.

You will find crumbled leaves and broken twigs in soil, too. You may see a busy ant or a ladybug or an earthworm. Many tiny creatures creep in soil. Some you can see. Some are too little to see. The worms and insects dig holes in soil and let air in. This helps to make the soil rich. They eat soil and when it passes through their bodies, it is broken into even tinier pieces. This makes the soil light and loose around the roots of young plants that grow in soil. There is water in soil, too, and bits of dead plants and animals. All these help to make the soil rich.

Most plants grow in this rich soil. If we had no soil, we would not have fruits or vegetables, cereals or bread. These foods come from plants. We would not have meat or milk or ice cream. These foods come from animals that eat plants.

What is at the North Pole?

When the needle of a compass points north, it is pointing to the North Pole. Do you know that there are really two North Poles? There is the *magnetic* North Pole. That is what makes your compass needle point north. There is also the *geographic* North Pole. That is farther north than any other place in the world. The magnetic North Pole lies about one thousand miles away from the geographic North Pole. Both North Poles lie in the Arctic ocean.

The Arctic ocean covers the North Pole region. It is very cold there in winter. Sometimes it is sixty-five degrees below zero! Ice and snow cover the Arctic ocean thickly. In winter this ice is so solid that dog sleds can travel over it. Light airplanes can land and take off safely. It is dark in the polar region from September to March, the period when the earth's tilt makes it impossible for sunlight to reach the North Pole.

Many animals live in the Arctic waters. You can find polar bears, walruses, whales, and seals there.

The first man to reach the North Pole was Robert E. Peary, an American explorer. He raised the United States flag there in 1909. The first men to fly to the North Pole were Admiral Richard E. Byrd and Floyd Bennett in 1926. In 1958 the atomic submarine USS *Nautilus* made the first undersea voyage under the Arctic ice. Today airplanes fly over the North Pole regularly.

Children Ask About Space Travel

I wonder

—where is space? If I were in space, what would I see?

—how does a spacecraft know where to go? Does an astronaut have a map that tells him?

—can a person on the moon see the earth? What does the earth look like from space?

—how can you walk in space?

—how do astronauts eat and sleep in space?

—what is the space shuttle? Why is it different from other spacecraft?

—could we live in a moon base? What are the other planets like?

—could I go to Mars or the other planets?

—could I be an astronaut or space scientist?

—*I wonder!*

Where is space?
Around the earth is a blanket of air called the atmosphere. Beyond the atmosphere, space begins. Space has no end, like an ocean without shores. We cannot imagine the immensity of space.

What is in space?
Moving through space are the planets, stars (including our own star, the sun), and smaller objects such as moons, comets, and meteors. Far from the earth among the distant stars are giant clouds of glowing gases and dust. There are also some man-made objects in space. These are the satellites and other spacecraft we have launched from earth to learn more about space.

What is it like in space?
It is icy cold in the huge black emptiness between the objects in space. There is no air in space. There is no heat or sound.

What is the earth?

The earth is one of nine planets that move around the sun. It is our home, the world on which we live.

What is the difference between a star and a planet?

A star shines with its own light. A planet gets its light from a star. We get our light from our star, the sun.

How big is the earth?

If you measure straight through the earth at the equator, the diameter of the earth is 7,926 miles. If you measure around the earth at the equator, the circumference is 24,902 miles. Compared to the sun, the earth is tiny. Just imagine that the earth is the size of a grain of sand. You would need to build a ball of more than a million grains of sand to show how much bigger the sun is!

What are the other planets like?

Most of the other planets would not make good homes. Some, like Mercury, are too hot. Others, like Jupiter, are covered with thick layers of poisonous gases. The most distant planets are bitterly cold.

What is the sun made of?

The sun is our nearest star. It is a huge ball of fiery gases, so hot that it glows with a brilliant light and gives off a vast amount of heat. Most of the gas in the sun is hydrogen and helium. It is so hot in the sun that any substance placed there would be boiled away instantly.

Why do we need the sun?

If the sun did not shine, the earth would be cold and dark. There would be no day and no seasons. No wind would blow because the sun warms the air and makes it move. The wind is moving air. The sun gives us heat and light. It warms the earth so plants can grow.

Without the sun, there would be no plants on earth. Green plants need light to help them make their own food. There would be no animals because animals eat plants or other animals that eat plants. The sun's light and heat make the earth a green, growing place on which we can live. We could not live without the sun.

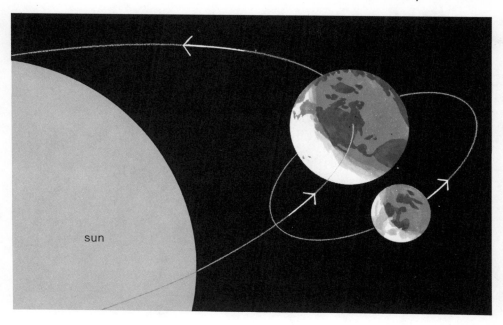

sun

What is the moon?

The moon is something like a small planet. It is a dry, lonely world where no winds blow and where nothing lives. There is no air and no water on the moon.

The moon is about 240,000 miles from the earth. It travels in a path, or orbit, around the earth. When a body such as the moon moves around a larger planet or a star, it is called a satellite. The moon takes about 28 days to make one trip around the earth. When we see the moon at different times of the month, it seems to change size. The reason for this is that the sun shines on different parts of the moon as the moon goes around the earth.

How did the moon get up in the sky?

Many scientists believe that both the earth and the moon are made of material that once came from a whirling cloud of hot gas around the sun. When this cooled, the earth and the moon were formed.

What is a satellite?

A satellite is an object that travels around a larger body in space. The moon moves in a path, or orbit, around the earth. It is earth's

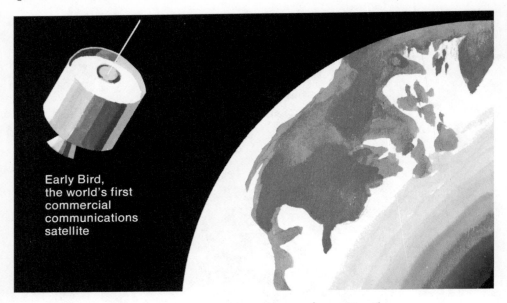

Early Bird,
the world's first
commercial
communications
satellite

only natural satellite. The planets are satellites of the sun. In 1957 the first man-made satellite was sent into space in an orbit around the earth. Today, many such satellites are in space. Many orbit the earth, while others travel around the sun. Some have even been put into orbit around other planets and the moon.

What holds a satellite in orbit? All objects in the universe pull on one another. Larger bodies pull more than small ones. It is this pull, called gravitation, that keeps a satellite from flying away from a larger body.

What do satellites do?

Satellites help scientists make many new discoveries about space and about the earth we live on. Weather satellites help weathermen know what the weather will be. Navigation satellites send radio messages so pilots in the air and sailors at sea can find their way safely in fog and rain. Communication satellites help link far places on earth by relaying radio messages, telephone calls, telegrams, and television programs.

Scientific satellites explore the secrets of space. As they fly by distant planets, they gather information that helps us understand more about our neighbors in space.

How are spacecraft launched?

Giant rockets are used to lift a spacecraft into space. Usually, the rockets are in two or three parts, or stages. When the rockets are put together, they form a launch vehicle. The spacecraft sits on top of the launch vehicle until it is in space. The rockets must be very powerful so that they can reach the speed needed for the spacecraft to go into orbit.

At lift-off, the fuel in the launch vehicle's first stage begins to burn quickly. The gases formed by the burning push against the launch vehicle and lift it into the air. When the first stage uses all its fuel after a few minutes, it drops away and the rockets in the second stage start firing. The launch escape system also drops off at this time.

After the second stage burns out and falls off, the third stage fires and carries the spacecraft into orbit. The third stage may be shut off and used later if the craft is to be sent toward the moon or a planet. But if the craft is to stay in earth orbit, the third stage is released.

Once the spacecraft is in space, it can use its own small rocket. This engine can be fired many times to help control the craft.

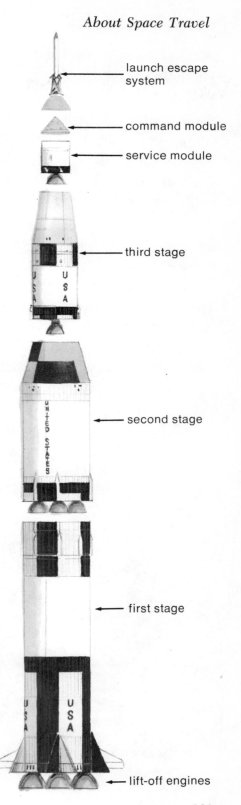

launch escape system

command module

service module

third stage

second stage

first stage

lift-off engines

123

What is a space trip like?

Far from earth, a spacecraft is moving swiftly through space. The lonely blackness of space is around it, but in the cabin of the command module, the astronauts are talking to earth. Voices from central control reach them. Voices from stations around the globe that are tracking their flight reach them, too.

From the windows of their cabin, the astronauts can see the bright ball that is earth. They can see blue oceans, brown land, and white clouds. They are too far away to see cities or people. If they were from another planet, they would not know there are people living on earth.

Inside the oxygen-pressurized cabin, the crew is busy. Many men and computers in central control on earth have planned carefully to put the spacecraft in orbit, but the navigator checks the course, too, with the stars and his computer. The craft can fly itself, but sometimes the pilot takes over control. He may guide the spacecraft into a new orbit or into a rendezvous, or meeting, with another spacecraft so they can link up.

This is how the astronauts went to the moon and returned to earth. Will astronauts some day visit Mars and other planets? Many scientists believe that they will, in the years ahead.

What is it like being weightless in space?

When a spacecraft is in space, its engines are shut off most of the time. The spacecraft is then in a condition called free fall. The craft and everything in it are weightless. If an astronaut lets go of a pencil, it doesn't fall but stays in mid-air.

The astronauts must move carefully. If one of them moves too quickly, he may float off his chair or bump into delicate instruments. When he sleeps, he must strap himself into his couch or sleeping hammock so that he won't float. Everything not in use must be fastened down to keep it from drifting around and possibly getting lost.

How does an astronaut eat in space?

When an astronaut is weightless in space, he cannot cook in an open pot because the food would float out. He cannot pour milk into a glass because there is no gravity to pull the milk down. Usually his food is prepared on earth. He may have a tube of mashed roast beef or applesauce he can squeeze into his mouth. He may have cereal cubes or freeze-dried powdery bacon in a plastic bag. By adding water, he can make these good to eat. He may have bite-sized steak he can eat by taking a drink of water. He can eat many foods in space!

What is a space station?

A space station is a large man-made satellite that orbits the earth. In it, astronauts and scientists can live, work, and study the earth and space. The Skylab placed in earth orbit by the United States was a space station. Teams of three astronauts lived for weeks at a time in the Skylab.

Future space stations may look like huge, slowly turning wheels. The turning would create a kind of gravity that pulls everything inside the station toward its outer rim. Because of this, the people in the space station would not have to live and work while being weightless.

How can astronauts work in space?

Imagine you are an astronaut and are helping to build a space station. The parts for the station were made on earth and placed in orbit by huge rockets. Because there is no weight in space, you float, just like the parts. A long cable fastens you to your spacecraft so that you do not float too far away. To put the parts of the space station together, you use special tools. For example, the wrench you use has two handles that you squeeze together to turn a bolt. You cannot use an ordinary wrench because there is no weight in space. If you tried, you might turn yourself instead of the bolt.

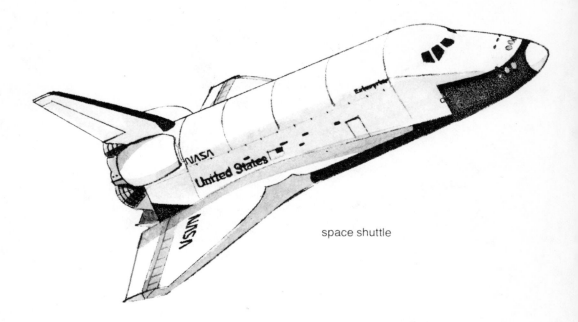

space shuttle

There is no heat or air in space. There is no sound because sound is carried on air waves. Your pressurized space suit keeps you warm. The oxygen pack on your back gives you air to breathe. You talk to others through the two-way radio in your helmet.

What is the space shuttle?

The space shuttle is a rocket-powered spacecraft that looks something like a jet airliner. It can carry scientists, satellites, and equipment into orbit around the earth. After remaining in orbit for a time, the shuttle returns to earth, where it lands like an airplane. The shuttle is then made ready for its next trip into space.

Could we build a base on the moon?

If you stood on the surface of the moon, you would see a lonely, desolate world. It would not look like a place where people could live and work for many months at a time. There is no air, water, or food on the moon. A single day lasts two weeks and is very hot. A night also lasts two weeks and is icy cold.

In spite of these difficulties, a moon base could be very useful. To astronomers, it would be a perfect place for an observatory.

Telescopes on earth must look at space through the thick layer of air that surrounds the earth. This often makes seeing stars and other objects very difficult. Since the moon has no air around it, it is a much better place from which to study space. Another use for a moon base would be as a port for spacecraft traveling between earth and other parts of the solar system.

A moon base would probably be made of a number of airtight buildings connected to one another. Perhaps the base would be mostly underground for protection against the sun and falling meteors. All the materials for building the base would have to be brought from earth. Oxygen, water, and food, as well as all other supplies, would also have to come from earth.

Later, the moon-base workers may begin taking oxygen and other chemicals from moon rocks. Perhaps some types of foods could be made from some of the chemicals. Other foods could be grown in special indoor gardens. The plants in these gardens would also provide some oxygen for breathing.

Electric or nuclear-powered vehicles could be used to explore distant parts of the moon. The vehicles would serve as living quarters while the explorers are away from the base. While working outside the base on the moon's surface, workers would wear pressurized and air-conditioned suits like those of the astronauts.

Can we go to other planets?

We have already sent unmanned spacecraft to study and explore several of the planets. In the 1970's, special spacecraft landed on Venus and Mars, while other craft photographed these and some of the other planets from space.

Mars will probably be the first planet visited by astronauts. It would take at least six months to get to Mars. There are still many problems to be solved about a space trip that long, but some day people from earth will walk on the red soil of Mars.

Can people live on other planets?

Of all the planets, Mars is most like the earth. It has four seasons and its day is about 24 hours long. But most of Mars is dry and its air has almost no oxygen. At night and in winter, Mars is very cold.

Mercury and Venus are far too hot. No plant or animal we know of could live there. Jupiter and the three other large planets have dense atmospheres of poisonous gases. These planets would have to be studied from space, or from bases on the moons of the planets. Some of these moons may be something like Mars.

Who made the first space flights?

On April 12, 1961, the first man went into orbit around the earth. He was a Russian, Yuri A. Gagarin. The first American to orbit the earth was John H. Glenn, Jr., on February 20, 1962. The first woman to go into space was Valentina Tereshkova, a Russian. She orbited the earth in 1963.

Since then many astronauts have orbited the earth and man has landed on the moon. The first men to set foot on the moon were the American astronauts Neil A. Armstrong and Edwin E. Aldrin, on July 20, 1969.

What does the earth look like from the moon?

Did you ever watch the moon rising in the night sky? If you were on the moon, you could see the earth rise like a huge blue and white marble above the moon's horizon.

The blue is the earth's oceans; the white, its clouds. You could also see the brown of the earth's land masses. No cities could be seen. Because the moon turns on its axis only once every 28 days, the earth would be in the sky for about two weeks.

Could I be an astronaut?

As we continue to explore the mysteries of space, more and more astronauts and space scientists will be needed. Perhaps one day you may be one of these space explorers. How can you get ready? What are some of the things you must know?

A person who plans to travel and work in space must know many things. Astronauts, for example, must be skilled in science and astronomy, and must know how to navigate by the stars and planets. Space scientists must be experts in geology or physics. Does this seem far away from the things you are studying in school now? It is not. Do you remember when you learned to add? You had to learn to add before you could learn to subtract, multiply, divide, and do fractions. The things you are learning in school today will help you learn the many things you need to know to help explore space.

Children Ask
About How Things Work

I wonder

—how does an airplane fly like a bird? A helicopter doesn't. It goes straight up in the air.

—how does a sailboat sail without an engine?

—how does a door open by itself? When I go to the department store, the door opens and closes. I don't have to touch it. Why?

—what makes a light go on?

—how does an alarm clock go off at the right time?

—how can stairs move? When I stand on the escalator, I go up and down, but I'm standing still.

—how can a camera take a picture?

—how does a thermometer tell how hot the temperature is?

—how does television work?

—*I wonder how!*

What makes an airplane fly? What is a jet plane?

An airplane's wings help it fly. The wings have a special shape. The wing top is curved. As the plane flies through the air, the air rushes over the curved top. The air moves so fast that it does not press hard. The wing bottom is flattened. Air moves more slowly over it. The air pushes it up. The air pushes the bottom of the wing up harder than it presses down on the top of the wing so the wing lifts in the air. As the wings lift, the plane rises, too.

When a plane flies, it is always moving. It has to keep moving so the air will flow over its wings. Its engine helps it keep moving. It gives the plane the power to move through the air.

A small plane usually has a gasoline engine. A big plane often has a jet engine and is called a jet plane. In a jet engine, air is squeezed, or compressed, and mixed with kerosene or other jet fuel. As this burns, it forms hot gases. The gases rush out of the rear end of the engine. As they rush out, the jet plane moves forward.

How does a helicopter rise straight up?

Watch a bird or a plane rise in the air. They do not fly straight up. A helicopter can go straight up and down. It can go backward and forward. It can go from side to side.

An airplane has wings. Its wings are at the sides. They help the airplane lift into the air and fly.

A helicopter has wings, too, but they are called rotors. They are above the body of the helicopter. The rotors are shaped like the wings of an airplane. They are curved on top and flattened on the bottom. They are thin and spin around and around in a circle.

As the helicopter's rotors spin around, they push against the air. They whirl faster and faster and push harder and harder. When the rotors spin fast enough, they lift the body of the helicopter straight up into the air. The body would spin with the rotors if the tail rotors did not spin, too. The tail rotors push the helicopter's tail away from the direction in which the overhead rotors are spinning. The tail rotors help keep the body of the helicopter steady.

Because a helicopter can go straight up or down, it does not need much space to take off or land. It can pick up passengers at an air field and land them on a rooftop. It can rescue people from a flood or from a mountaintop or a spot in the jungle. It can take off and land in many places that are too small for an airplane.

How does a submarine go under water?

A submarine looks something like a huge whale. It can travel on top of the water and under water. How can it go up and down?

The main wall, or hull, of a submarine is really two walls. In the space between the walls are huge tanks. Some hold fuel. Others hold air. In the bottom of each air tank is a tiny door, called a valve. At the top of each air tank is another valve.

When the submarine captain wants the submarine to go down, or submerge, the top valves are opened. The air escapes through these valves. The bottom valves are opened, too. Water enters through them. As the tanks fill with water, the submarine sinks below the water.

When the captain wants the submarine to go up, or surface, the top valves are closed. Air is blown into the tanks. The air has been squeezed, or compressed, in huge metal bottles. As the air rushes into the tanks, it pushes the water out. When the tanks are filled with air, the submarine rises to the top of the water because air is lighter than water.

Some submarines use diesel engines to travel on top of the water. These engines need air so they cannot work under water. These submarines use electric batteries under water. Other submarines use atomic engines that do not need air. They can go on top of the water and under water for a long time.

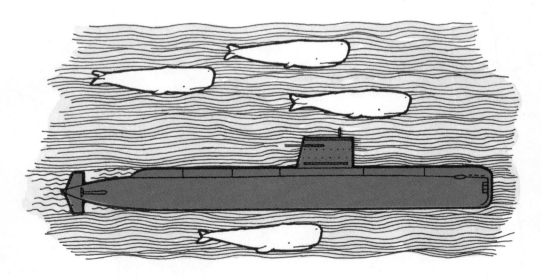

What makes a sailboat go?

The wind makes a sailboat go. A tall pole, or mast, holds the mainsail. A smaller sail ahead of the mast is the jib. The wind pushes the sails and the sailboat moves through the water.

The centerboard helps keep the boat steady and reduces the sideways push of the wind. The tiller is connected to the rudder under the boat. When you move the tiller, the rudder moves. This helps you steer the boat.

The mainsail has slots for thin sticks, called battens. They make the sail stiff so the wind can push it. A rope, or line, called a sheet lets the sail out or pulls it in so you can set it where it will catch the wind. When sailed correctly, a boat will tip just enough to let any extra wind slide over the sail.

When the wind blows from behind the boat, it pushes the boat ahead. The boat is running with the wind. When the wind is from the side, the boat is on a beam reach.

If the wind is from the front, you must beat or zigzag your way into the wind. If the boat heads right into the wind, the sail shakes and the boat stands still. This is called luffing.

Sailing is fun!

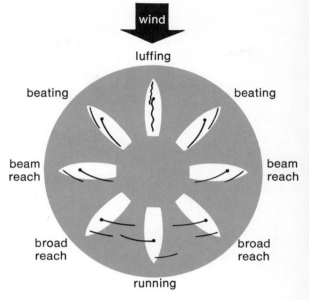

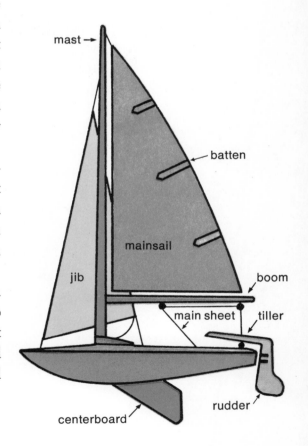

137

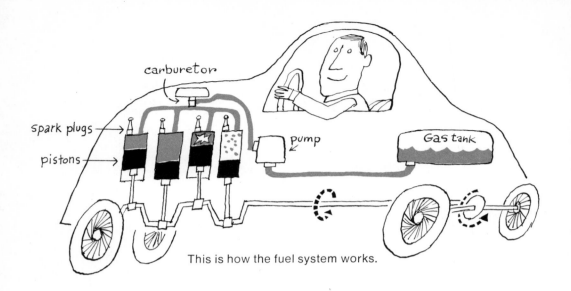

This is how the fuel system works.

What makes an automobile go?

The engine makes an automobile go. The engine needs gasoline. The gasoline is in the gas tank. A long tube, or gas line, runs under the car from the gas tank to the engine. The fuel pump sucks gasoline from the gas tank and through the gas line to the carburetor. The carburetor mixes the gasoline with air and the mixture is drawn into the cylinders. Inside the cylinders are pistons that slide up and down. When the pistons go up, they push the gasoline and air mixture into a small space. Electric sparks from the spark plugs make the mixture burn quickly. This makes the pistons go down hard. Metal rods connect the pistons to the crankshaft. As the pistons and rods go up and down, they make the crankshaft turn round and round. They give it power that runs through the transmission to the rear or front wheels of the automobile. The car goes.

How does a car start? The driver closes a switch, usually by turning the ignition key as far as it will go. The switch sends electricity from the battery to the starter motor. The motor turns the crankshaft, causing the engine to start.

Most car engines need water. When the fuel in the cylinders burns, it gets very hot. If it gets too hot, the engine cannot work. To keep the engine from getting too hot, water is pumped through passages around the cylinders. The water absorbs the heat and runs back to the radiator. There the water is cooled by air that is drawn through the radiator by a fan at the front of the engine. The cool water goes back to the cylinders. It makes this circle over and over.

138

What makes a train go?

A train is roaring by on the railroad tracks. Can you count the cars? A passenger train has coaches where people ride. It sometimes has sleeping cars and dining cars, too. It is like a hotel on wheels. A freight train pulls many kinds of loads. It has many cars, too. When the freight conductor sits in his caboose, or office, he can talk by two-way radio to his engineer who may be fifty cars away!

Because a train has so many cars, it needs a heavy, powerful engine to pull it. A train engine is called a locomotive. Most trains today have diesel-electric locomotives. This kind of locomotive has a diesel engine and electric motors.

In a diesel engine, a piston moves down into a cylinder and sucks air in through an open valve. The piston is connected by an arm to the crankshaft. The crankshaft turns and pushes the piston up. This closes the valve and squeezes, or compresses, the air. The air becomes very hot. Then oil fuel is forced into the cylinder. The heat makes it catch fire. As it burns, it turns into gas. The gas explodes and pushes the piston down again. As the piston moves, it turns the crankshaft.

A diesel engine does not turn the wheels of a train. It turns an electric generator that makes electricity for the electric motors. The electric motors make the wheels of the train roll.

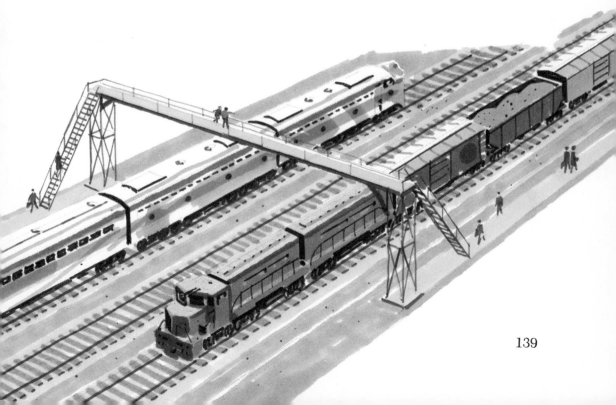

How can stairs move?

A moving stairway is called an escalator. The stairs are attached to an endless chain that moves around toothed wheels at the top and bottom. The chain looks something like a bicycle chain except the toothed wheels are both the same size. A heavy electric motor is geared to the top wheel. The motor makes the stairs move.

The stairs can move up or down. When moving down, the stairs fold into flat sections as they reach the bottom. They slide under a flat plate and are pulled up to the top by the chain. At the top they slide out from under a plate and unfold to form stairs again.

There is a railing on each side of the stairs. It moves at the same speed as the stairs.

You can see escalators in department stores, airline terminals, and other public places. In some places, there are moving sidewalks. They are made up of plates like those in an escalator except that they are always flat.

What makes a door open by itself?

Sometimes when you go to a department store, you walk up to the door and it swings open. You did not touch the door. What made it open? Electricity made it open. When you came near the door, you passed through a beam of light or stepped on something that made the electricity go on.

The electricity started an electric motor. The motor pumped oil through hoses, and the oil pushed a lever that swung the door open.

After you passed through the door, the electricity stopped, so the electric motor stopped, too. The oil stopped pushing. A spring made the door close.

What makes a door go round and round?

Did you ever go round and round in a revolving door? This kind of door is really four doors in one. Two of the doors are always closed. Two of the doors are open.

In the middle of the four doors is a pin. When you push one of the doors, the pin turns in holes in the floor and the ceiling. The doors turn round and round.

What makes a light go on?

You pull a string or snap on a wall switch and a light goes on. What did you do? You started electricity moving along wires.

Electric wires run to all parts of your house. They connect with wires at an electric power plant. When you switch on a light, the switch acts as a bridge over which electricity moves to the wires that are connected to the light bulb.

Inside the light bulb is a thin, coiled wire called a filament. When electricity flows through the filament, it becomes white hot and glows. There is light.

A light bulb can give light for a long time. The filament is made of a metal called tungsten. Tungsten will not melt except at a very high temperature.

To protect the filament, all air was removed from the bulb before the filament was placed inside it. Without air, the filament can burn longer. Special gases that do not burn were also placed inside the bulb. These, too, help keep the filament from burning away. Then the glass bulb was sealed so no air could get in.

What makes an alarm clock ring at the right time?

When do you want an alarm clock to ring? You move a hand on the clock to the right time. Inside the clock, a pointer presses a turning alarm wheel down. The wheel presses a tiny lever down. This stops a tiny striker from hitting the clock bell. When the right time comes, the pointer drops into a groove on the alarm wheel. The wheel springs up, and the tiny lever springs up, too. The striker hits the clock bell. The alarm clock rings.

What makes a doorbell ring?

When you press a doorbell button, electricity moves through the wire that connects the button to the doorbell. Then it moves to an electric magnet, or electromagnet, inside the bell box. The magnet pulls a clapper away from a screw and pushes it toward the bell. The clapper strikes the bell. The doorbell rings.

As soon as the clapper moves away from the screw, the electricity stops. After the clapper strikes the bell, a spring makes the clapper rebound against the screw. The electricity starts again. As long as you press the doorbell button, the clapper keeps moving.

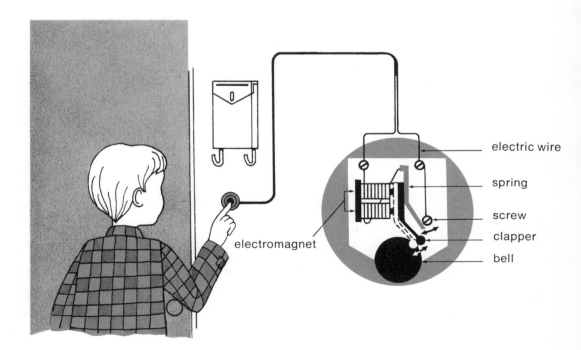

electric wire

spring

screw

clapper

bell

electromagnet

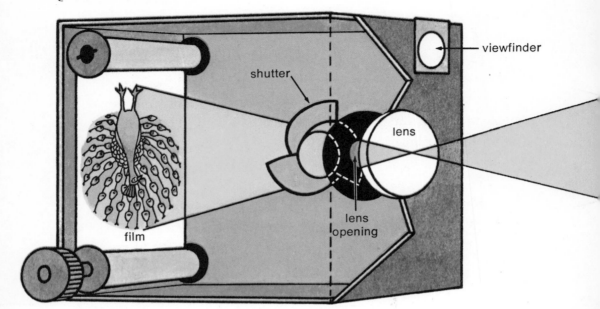

How does a camera take a picture?

It is fun to take pictures with a camera. It is fun, too, later to look at the pictures. There you are at the beach or at a party or perhaps opening presents under the Christmas tree. As you look at the pictures, you enjoy your happy times all over again.

There are many kinds of cameras. Some are little. Some are big. Some are easy to use, and some are not. But all cameras are alike in some ways.

A camera has a box that is dark inside.

It has an opening where light can enter and strike the film at the back of the camera.

It has a lens. A lens is a curved piece of glass. It makes the light form an upside-down picture, or image, inside the camera.

A camera has a shutter. The shutter opens and closes very quickly. It lets light into the camera and then shuts it out.

A camera uses film. Usually the film is a long strip of plastic that is coated with chemicals, that have silver in them. When light from the lens hits the film, the silver is changed. You cannot see this change until the film is put through a bath of special chemicals, or developed. Then you see an image on the film.

Now let's take a picture with a box camera. You load the camera with film. Then you look through the viewfinder. The viewfinder will show you the picture the camera will take.

Press the button on the camera. This makes the shutter open for just a fraction of a second before it closes. While the shutter is open, light enters the camera. Light strikes the film at the back of the camera. An image forms on the film.

Now turn the film knob. This makes the film move, or advance, so new film is ready for a new picture.

You can take black-and-white pictures. If you use color film, you can take color pictures. You can take pictures outdoors. You can take pictures indoors, too, if you use flash bulbs or flash cubes.

You can take better and better pictures if you follow these rules.

Hold your camera steady when you take a picture. Press the button slowly. This will help you take sharp, not blurred, pictures.

Don't go too close. When you use a box camera, stay about six feet away. This will help you take sharper pictures, too.

Point the camera away from the sun when you take a picture out-doors. Let the sunlight fall on the picture you are taking.

Have fun taking pictures with your camera!

How does a telephone work?

Do you know that your voice makes sound waves? When you talk into a tin-can telephone, the sound waves make the bottom of the can move in and out, or vibrate. The string stretched tightly between your can and your friend's can vibrates, too. It makes the bottom of his can move in and out and push against the air. This makes sound waves. The sound waves strike his ear, and he hears your voice.

A real telephone is connected to wires over which electricity moves. Behind the mouthpiece is a thin metal plate, or diaphragm. Behind the diaphragm are thousands of tiny carbon grains. When you pick up a telephone, electricity begins moving through the carbon. When you speak into the mouthpiece, the sound waves of your voice make the diaphragm move back and forth. As it vibrates, it presses against the carbon grains and squeezes them tightly together, then lets them move apart. When the carbon is pressed together, more electricity can flow through it. The sound waves of your voice are sent out, or transmitted, by this electric current.

Telephone wires carry the electric current to the receiver of another telephone. In the receiver, the current passes through an electromagnet to a thin plate. This makes the thin plate vibrate and change the electric current back into the sounds of your voice. Your voice comes out of the telephone receiver!

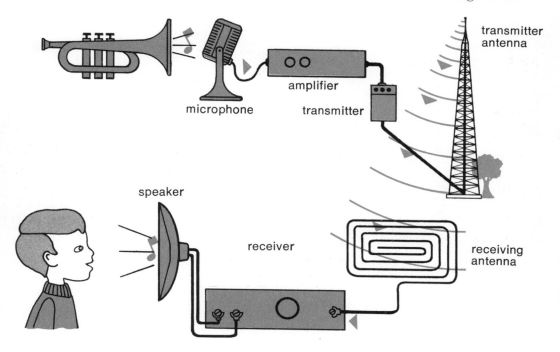

transmitter antenna

amplifier

microphone   transmitter

speaker

receiver   receiving antenna

How does radio work?

There is music in the air. You can hear the music, but you cannot see who is making it because the music is coming from your radio. How does the music reach you?

At the radio broadcasting studio, a man is playing a trumpet in front of a microphone. The microphone changes the sound waves from the trumpet into electrical waves, or electric current. Then the electric current goes to a control room at the studio where transistors make it stronger, or amplify it. Now the electric current goes to a transmitter. There it is combined with carrier waves and made stronger and changes into radio waves. The transmitter antenna sends the radio waves rippling out into the air.

When the radio waves touch the antenna of your radio set, or receiver, a tiny electric current flows into your set. Your tuner picks out the radio program you want to hear. Then the radio waves are changed back into electric waves and go to the loudspeaker. It changes them back into sound waves. You hear music.

Television brings you music and other sounds in the same way.

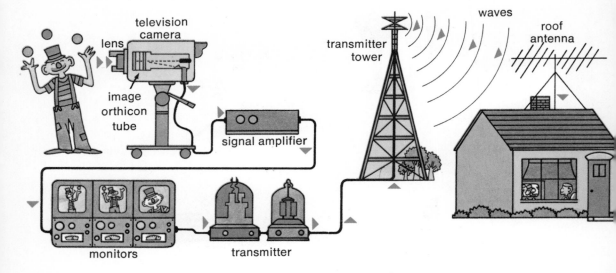

How does television work?

In a television studio miles away from your home, a clown juggles balls. You can see him juggling the balls on your television screen. It seems like magic, but it is not magic.

In the television studio, a camera is pointed at the clown. The camera does not use film. It is a television camera that uses electrons to make pictures. The camera lens, a curved piece of glass, bends light to bring a picture of the clown to a camera tube inside the camera. Usually this is an image orthicon tube. This tube has a tiny postage-stamp size screen, called a photoscreen. Light goes through the lens and hits the screen, which gives off electrons. Electrons are tiny jots of electricity. Behind the photoscreen is another screen, called a target. The target screen collects the electrons in a pattern of the picture on the photoscreen. Behind the target is an electron gun which shoots more electrons at the back of the screen. The gun sprays the target very fast from left to right, top to bottom. This is called scanning. The electron gun makes 525 sweeps of the target for every picture.

In scanning, the stream of electrons from the electron gun searches for electrons that hit the front of the target to find out how many hit each part. Then it bounces back to the rear of the camera tube with the messages. Near the electron gun is a small metal plate, called a collecting plate. It gathers the returning stream of electrons. This stream is called a signal.

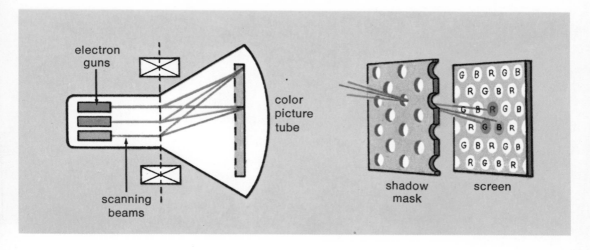

electron guns

color picture tube

scanning beams

shadow mask

screen

G B R G B
R G B R
G B R G B
R G B R
G B R G B
R G B R

The picture signal is very weak, so it goes through an amplifier that makes it stronger.

Often three cameras are taking pictures in a studio. Each one sends a signal to the television control room. The picture from each camera is seen on a small television set, called a monitor. The director looks at all the pictures and picks the one he wants to send to your home. That signal goes by wires to the transmitter. On top of a tall tower is a big antenna which spreads the signals out through the air. The signal moves like a wave. The antenna of your television set pulls the signal from the air and sends it to your set. Transistors in your set make the signal stronger and then send it to the picture tube.

Like the camera tube, your picture tube has an electron gun at the back end. The gun changes the signal back into electrons and sprays, or scans, the television screen you watch. Tiny dots glow on the screen. The scanning makes the picture you see.

Just three colors make your color television picture. The camera has three tubes, one for each color: red, blue, green. Your color set has three electron guns. They shoot electrons at a metal plate, called a shadow mask, that has thousands of tiny holes. The screen behind it has the same number of groups of color dots of red, blue, and green. When the electrons from each gun hit the screen, dots of one of the colors glow. All the glowing colors mix together to make the color picture on your television screen.

How does a thermometer work?

If the temperature goes up to a hundred or higher, you know it is hot! The thermometer tells you exactly how hot it is.

A thermometer can tell you how hot or cold the weather is. A thermometer can tell you if you have a fever or not. It measures heat and cold.

Usually a thermometer is just a glass tube with a glass bulb at one end. The tube is filled with a liquid and sealed. In a weather thermometer, the liquid is usually alcohol because alcohol freezes only at a very low temperature.

Most medical thermometers are filled with mercury because it can show heat or cold more exactly.

When the alcohol or mercury in a thermometer gets hot, it swells, or expands. It rises in the hollow glass tube. When the alcohol or mercury cools, it shrinks, or contracts, down toward the bulb.

If you look at a thermometer and see a silver line, there is mercury inside the glass tube. If alcohol is in the tube, it may be colored red or blue to make it easy to see.

You will see numbers on the thermometer, too. They will tell you exactly what the measurement of heat or cold is. What does your thermometer show?

How can an air conditioner work?

Outside it is hot. As you walk down the street, your hair clings damply to your forehead and little beads of perspiration roll down your face. Then a breeze blows and the tiny drops of perspiration, which are mostly water, dry up, or evaporate. You feel cooler. What made the tiny drops of water evaporate? The air did.

An air conditioner can cool a room by making a liquid evaporate, too. Inside the air conditioner is a special liquid that goes into a metal coil, called a cooling coil. The liquid evaporates quickly there and forms a gas that spreads through the coil. As the liquid evaporates, it makes the coil cooler. Then a fan draws warm air from the room into the air conditioner. The coil cools the air, and then the air is pushed back into the room. The air cools the room.

Next a pump sucks the gas out of the cooling coil. It squeezes the gas into a smaller space and this makes the gas hot. The gas goes to a coiled tube that takes in air from outdoors. Even if the outside air is very warm, it is still cooler than the hot gas in the tube. The air cools the tube and the gas inside the tube gets cooler, too. As the gas cools, it changes back into liquid and flows back into the cooling coil in the air conditioner.

Then it all begins again. Over and over again warm air goes into the air conditioner. Cool air comes out. The air cools the room. Outside it is hot, but the room is cool and comfortable.

151

Children Ask
About What People Do

Everywhere I go, I see people working, and I wonder

—what do they really do?

—what does a fireman do when he fights a fire?

—what does a pilot do when he flies a plane?

—what do all the people in a bank and at the post office and in a library do?

—what does a weatherman do? How does he find out if it is going to rain or snow?

—what do doctors and nurses do? What do all the other people in a hospital do?

—who gets the news for the newspapers? How do they do it?

—who makes the television shows? What do they do?

—what would I do if I were a policeman? Would I like doing it?

—I wonder!

What does a weatherman do?

A weatherman may be at a weather station in the frozen north or on a mountaintop or near your home. He may be in a plane flying into a big storm, called a hurricane. What is he doing? He is watching the weather signs so planes in the air, ships at sea, farmers on land, and you, too, can know what the weather will be.

Will the day be sunny or is a big storm coming? A weatherman uses many instruments to find out. Is the air hot or cold? Is the air pressure high or low? If it is high, the weather probably will be clear. If it is low, the day may be stormy or cloudy. How much moisture is in the air? How fast is the wind blowing and from what direction? His instruments tell him. Weather balloons help him, too. Weather satellites in space tell him about the air over the earth.

Then a weatherman makes a map to show what the weather will be all over the country, and the weather news goes to radio and television stations and newspapers. They tell you what the weather will be!

What do postal workers do?

Your letter carrier brings you letters and valentines. He brings you birthday packages and magazines, too. He brings you your mail. How does he get your mail? Many persons work together to bring you a letter.

When your friend sends you a letter, she puts your name, address, and a stamp on the envelope. She drops the letter in a mailbox.

A letter carrier takes all the mail from the mailbox and puts it on a truck. The truck takes the mail to the post office.

There other workers sort all the letters and packages. Mail for each town and each state is put in separate piles. Mail that is going to France or Japan or other countries is sorted, too.

Most mail is put on trucks or airplanes. Some mail goes by trains, by mail boats, or by ships on the sea.

When your letter comes to your post office, it is put with other mail for your street. Your letter carrier puts it in his mailbag. He brings you your letter.

When you go to the post office, a clerk may sell you stamps or take the package you want to send. If there were no postal workers, could you get or send a letter?

What does a fireman do?

Listen! A siren is blasting the air. A fire engine is racing down the street. If you follow, you will see red flames and gray, billowing smoke. A building is burning.

The fire engine stops, and the firemen jump off. They attach a short hose to a fire hydrant and connect it to a pump on the fire truck. They attach other hoses to the truck and turn on the water. Soon the water pumps out. Some of the firemen hold the hoses tight and aim the water at the flames. Other firemen go into the building. They bring out people. They fight to put out the fire.

Firemen fight fires in buildings. Firemen on fire boats fight fires on rivers and lakes, too.

Firemen also fight forest fires. They are called smoke jumpers, and they parachute from helicopters to help put out the fires.

Who works in a bank?

When you go into a bank, you will see a man in uniform. He is the bank guard. He helps keep the money in a bank safe. He helps people who come into the bank, too.

Did you know that a bank will pay you to keep your money there? This payment is called interest and you will receive it every few months if you have a savings account. Ask the guard how to open a savings account and he will take you to a person seated at a desk.

The person at the desk will take your money and give you a little bank book, or passbook. The passbook has your name and a number on it. It shows exactly how much money you have in the bank.

To put more money in the bank or take money out, you go to the sign that says Savings. Behind the counter is a man or woman who will help you. This is the bank clerk, or bank teller. The bank teller takes your money and enters the amount in your passbook. The teller does this when you take money out, too.

Banks also have checking accounts. A checking account is used to keep money safe until you need to spend it. Then you write a check. Next time your mother writes a check, ask her if you may see it.

What does a policeman do?

At a busy corner, a policeman is directing traffic. When he holds up his hand or blows his whistle, some cars stop, others go. He is a traffic policeman.

Some traffic policemen do not stand at street corners. They are in helicopters, watching the traffic on the highways below. If they see a speeding car, they use their two-way radio to call a police car on the ground. The police car chases the speeder to catch him before he can cause an accident.

There are many kinds of policemen. Once, long ago, watchmen walked about a city at night. Each hour they would call out the time, like this: "Ten o'clock and all is well!" Today our policemen watch over our towns and cities during the day and night. Many policemen have a certain section of a city to watch over. This is their beat. Usually they do not walk their beats. They drive around in police cars with flashing lights on top. They watch to see that the people, houses, and stores are safe. If there is trouble, they try to stop it. If they need help, they call their police station on their two-way radio. The police station can call them, too, to send them to a trouble spot, and they can drive there swiftly.

Many policewomen also help keep our towns and cities safe. Some work with boys and girls who are in trouble. They try to help them learn how to live happily and safely.

Many policemen and policewomen wear uniforms. Others do not. They are police detectives. If there is a robbery or other crime, they try to find out who did it and catch the criminals.

The police photographer helps them. When there is a crime, he takes pictures of the place where it happened. Then the police detectives can study the picture to find clues to what happened. Sometimes the picture may be used as evidence to prove if a person is innocent or guilty.

In the police laboratory, men work to help solve crimes, too. They check fingerprints. They check the markings on bullets to find out from what gun the bullets were fired. They take many kinds of tests to help solve a crime.

Some policemen work for towns or cities. Others work for a state. They are state police, or state troopers. Often they patrol the highways to help keep the people driving on them safe.

Our policemen risk danger to watch over us. How can we help them? We can all try to obey the laws and be good citizens.

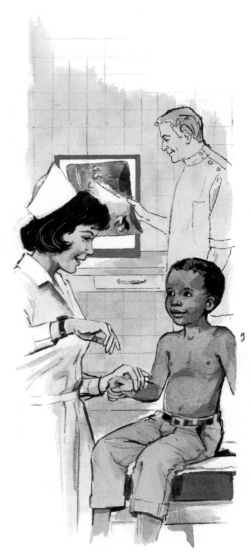

What does a nurse do?

When you go to a doctor's office, a nurse takes your temperature. She puts her finger on a pulse in your wrist to find out how fast it is beating. She times the beat with the second hand on her watch. She weighs you. She helps you get ready for the doctor.

Many nurses work in hospitals. When a doctor operates to make somebody well, nurses help him. They take care of many kinds of sick people, too. They take care of mothers and new babies.

Some nurses do not work in a doctor's office or in a hospital. If somebody is sick at home, these nurses come to take care of the sick person and help him get well.

Some nurses are school nurses. Did a nurse ever come to your school? What did she do? School nurses help children in school keep healthy and strong.

A nurse is not a soldier or a sailor, but there are nurses in the army, the navy, the air force, and the marines. Like the other nurses, they help the doctors take care of sick or hurt people and make them well.

Most nurses are women. But men can be nurses, too. Most male nurses work in hospitals or on emergency teams.

What does a doctor do?

A doctor can set a broken arm so it will heal and be strong and straight again. He can help cure measles or a sore throat and many other illnesses. He helps sick people get well.

He helps prevent illnesses, too. Did you ever go to the doctor for a vaccination? A vaccination can keep you from catching a sickness such as the measles. How often do you go to your doctor for a checkup? When you go regularly, your doctor helps you stay well.

Many doctors work in hospitals. Some operate on sick people to make them well. Others take care of many kinds of sick people. Other hospital workers help them. Some make laboratory tests to find out why people are sick. Some take X-ray pictures to find out. Nurses help the doctors, too.

Some doctors do a special kind of work. An eye doctor tests your eyes to find out if you need to wear glasses to see well. If you need glasses, he writes an order, or prescription, for the right kind of glasses. Eye doctors and others who do special kinds of work are called specialists.

Once, almost all doctors were men. Today, there are many women doctors as well.

Who works at an airport?

An airport is a busy, exciting place. Out on the field, planes land and take off. Inside the airport terminal, passengers are buying tickets from the ticket sellers. Other passengers are watching as their baggage is weighed. Still other passengers sit in chairs near the windows and watch the planes on the field.

The airport workers are always busy, but they are not too busy to help people and answer their questions. A hostess smiles at a little girl and tells her about the airport.

Suddenly a loudspeaker calls, "Flight 396 now loading!"

Passengers start hurrying toward the field so they can go on board the plane.

Outside on the field, it is busy, too. Mechanics are checking a plane to make sure it is working well before it takes off. A truck driver delivers food to another plane for the passengers to eat. Trucks carry baggage and mail to load on planes. Other trucks carry fuel out to the planes. Men load the fuel in the fuel tanks.

Where is the plane for Flight 396? Men are wheeling a stairway up to that plane. Now the stairway reaches high to the plane's door. As the passengers go up the stairway, a stewardess stands in the doorway to welcome them on board.

In the airline dispatch department, it is also busy. A weatherman is making a weather map to show the latest weather reports. A pilot is looking at the weather map so he can plan his flight safely.

High in the air-traffic control tower, it is even busier. Some of of the men there look at radar screens. White dots on the screen show where all nearby planes are, and how high they are and how fast they are flying. Other men look out at the field where they can see the planes coming in and taking off. They can talk to the pilots of the planes by radio.

Did you ever watch a traffic policeman direct traffic at a busy street corner? The men in the control tower direct traffic, too, but they direct planes, not automobiles. They tell the pilots when a runway is clear and it is safe for a plane to take off. They tell the pilots when it is safe to land. Sometimes they tell a pilot that he must wait to land. Then the pilot flies his plane around in huge circles, called a holding pattern, until the control tower tells him he can land.

A pilot flies a plane. His co-pilot helps him fly the plane. The flight engineer on the plane checks all the equipment to make sure that it is working well. The stewardesses or flight attendants serve the passengers food and help make them comfortable as they fly.

All the busy people at an airport help the planes fly, too.

What do people do on a newspaper?

There is a fire in your town. A newspaper reporter and photographer go to the fire. The photographer takes pictures of the flames with his camera. The reporter talks to many people to find out how the fire started and how much damage was done. Then they return to the newspaper office. The photographer turns his film over to the photo department. It is developed and made into pictures by men who work in a dark room. The reporter types his story and gives it to the copy editors.

The copy editors sit around a horse-shoe-shaped table called the copy desk. They read the fire story to make sure it is told in the right way. They write a headline for it. Then the story goes to the city editor who decides where it will go in the newspaper. He may talk about this with the managing editor who knows all the stories the newspaper will print that day.

Another man, called a state or cable editor, looks at the teletype machines. They look like typewriters, but they print stories that are typed by people in other cities. Pictures that come from other cities are printed on a machine called a facsimile printer. Like the fire story, the news stories from the teletype machines go to the copy desk for

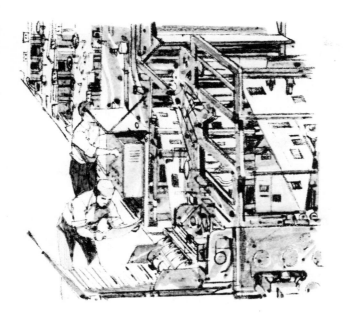

checking, correction, and headlines.

A newspaper office is busy and noisy. Telephones ring as reporters call in to tell news stories to men at typewriters. These men are called rewritemen. They write stories for reporters who do not have time to come back to the office.

After the news stories are written and checked, they are ready to be set in type. This is done either by a typesetter using a keyboard or by an automatic machine that "reads" what the reporters have written. The type consists either of raised letters on pieces of metal or flat letters printed by photography on film or paper. The type is checked by men and women called proofreaders.

At the same time, the pictures are made into halftones. A halftone consists of thousands of tiny dots on a metal plate or piece of photographic film.

The type and halftones are put together into pages. Next, exact copies of the type and halftones are made on metal plates. The plates are sent to the printing press. Paper and ink are pressed over them. The newspaper is printed.

A delivery boy or girl carries the paper to your home or you buy it at a drugstore or newstand. You read all about the fire!

Who works in a library?

Do you think people who work in a library sit and read storybooks all day? Next time you go to a library, watch and see how many different things a librarian does.

A librarian types your library card so you can take out books.

A librarian checks out the books you take from the library.

A librarian checks in the books you bring back.

Page boys and page girls stack the books on carts and wheel them to the children's room or the art room or the science room or any other room where the books belong. Then the pages put the books back on the shelves in the right places. They help make it easy for you to find the books when you want them.

Do you need to find a special book so you can do your homework? You go to the librarian at her desk. She tries to help you find it.

Sometimes you do not need a book. You need a picture. You go to the art room. There are many art books there. There are files and files of pictures, too. The librarian helps you find the picture you need.

In the music room, there are records you can play. You can take out the records on your card, too. The librarian helps you do it.

Many libraries have storytelling time. Sometimes you take your little sister or brother. Sometimes you go with your best friend. The librarian tells or reads a story, and it is fun.

Some libraries show movies. The movie may be about children in other lands. It may be a fairy tale or animal story. Who runs the movie projector? The librarian!

Librarians work in many kinds of libraries. Some libraries are big and have many different rooms. Some are small. One room can be a library, and the librarian will help you find books to read.

Some libraries move on wheels! They are called bookmobiles. The books are on shelves in a kind of truck. A librarian drives the bookmobile to a place where there is no other library. Children and grown-ups come to take books.

A bookmobile librarian may drive many miles to many places before she returns to the big library from which she gets her books.

Many librarians work in public libraries where everyone may come to take books.

Other librarians work in schools. Does your school have a library? Did you ever help the librarian? It is a good way to find out what librarians do.

Who works at a television station?

When you sit before your television set at home, you see only a very few of the people who work in the television station. You see the dancers and singers, the storytellers, the newsmen. You see the actors. These people do their work *in front* of the camera. They are called performers. The camera takes their pictures so you can watch them at home. But there are many people who work *behind* the camera, people you do not see.

The cameraman is very important. He takes the pictures you watch on your television screen. He is in the studio with the actors, the singers, the dancers. Also in the studio are other men and women, called technicians.

One man works the boom mike, which is a microphone on a long pole. Another man handles the lights. Sometimes he is called a gaffer. The camera needs light to take pictures.

A floor director tells the actors when to move and when to speak. He tells them when to turn to face another camera. A prop man makes sure that all the things needed for the program are in the studio. He looks after chairs and other furniture and all the things you see on your television screen.

Many other people work together to bring the television program to your screen. In the control room, the director sits at a table with many small televison sets, called monitors. On each monitor is a picture from a different camera in the studio. The director looks at all the pictures and chooses which picture to send to your home. He also tells the cameramen in the studio where to move to take the pictures. He works with the floor director to tell the actors when and where to move. His assistant director helps him.

At the control panel, a man listens to the sound coming from the studio and decides whether to make it softer or louder. He and many other workers we do not see help bring us our television programs.

169

Who works in a school?

If somebody asked you who works in a school, what would you say?

Teachers!

Your classroom teacher teaches you reading. She teaches you to add and subtract and use numbers. She teaches you science. Sometimes you do scientific experiments. Sometimes you may go outdoors for nature study. You learn about your own country and its history and other countries, too.

Some teachers are your special teachers. Your physical education teacher teaches you gym. You may have an art or music teacher, too. In some schools, there is a teacher for French or Spanish.

Many schools also have a teacher who tests children to see how well they are learning. She is called an adjustment teacher.

Who else works in a school?

The principal is in charge of a school. He helps the teachers plan what they will teach. He watches over the school to see that all the teachers and all the children are doing well.

The assistant principal helps the principal.

A clerk helps the principal, too. She types letters and orders paper and chalk and other supplies the school needs.

A school librarian works in the school library. When your class goes to the library, what do you do? What do you learn? How does the school librarian help you?

Who keeps your school warm and safe and comfortable? The school janitor, or school custodian, helps take care of the school building. The school engineer helps keep it warm and comfortable.

How often does a school nurse visit your school? Who comes to test your eyes and ears to make sure you are seeing and hearing well? All these people, too, work for children in school. They help to keep you healthy and strong.

Men from the fire department inspect your school to make sure it is safe. They tell you the fire safety rules. You have a fire drill to teach you what to do if there is a fire. Then you can get out safely.

A policeman visits your school, too. Some schools call this policeman Officer Friendly. He tells all the children how they can live safely and happily by following good rules.

Who else works in a school? You do!

As you study and learn, you are finding out what you will want to be when you grow up. You are learning many things you will need to know when you are grown up.

Children Ask
About This and That

I wonder

—what makes popcorn pop?

—are black cats really unlucky? My kitten is all black. She purrs and purrs and plays with a ball. She is the funniest kitten. How can she be unlucky?

—what makes an echo? I stood on a hill and called my name, and my name called back and back at me.

—why is ice slippery?

—what makes a jumping bean jump?

—why can't I see through a mirror? I can see through a window.

—what is the biggest thing in the world?

—how can a magnifying glass make fire?

—what is the most wonderful thing in the world?

—I wonder!

What makes a jumping bean jump?
A tiny caterpillar inside the bean makes it jump. A moth lays an egg in one of the three cells of a seed pod that grows on a Mexican plant. The egg hatches into a caterpillar that begins to eat the food inside the seed pod, or bean. It spins a silk web around itself. As the caterpillar grows, it gets heavy. In time the seed pod falls to the ground and splits open. When the caterpillar moves, the bean jumps. After a while the caterpillar changes into a moth and comes out of the bean.

What makes popcorn pop?
When you put corn into a popper, the kernel shells are hard. Inside each kernel is a soft part that has tiny drops of water in it. When you hold the kernels over a fire, this water turns to steam. The steam presses against the hard shells of the kernels until it gets so hot, it bursts out. The fluffy white parts puff out.

174

Where does wood go when it burns?

Did you ever sit around a fireplace and watch a log of wood burning? After a while, there is nothing left but a heap of gray ashes. Where did the wood go?

Some of the log went up the chimney in smoke. The rest of the log was very hot. As it burned, it mixed with air and changed into very hot, invisible gases. The hot gases were so light they flew away up the chimney.

What makes iron nails rusty?

If you leave a box of iron nails out in the rain over night, they probably will be rusty next day. The wet rain and the air make the iron rust.

Air has oxygen in it. When oxygen, water, and iron come together, a chemical change takes place. They make rust.

You can protect iron objects from rust if you oil or grease them. The oil or grease makes a coating, or film, that oxygen and water cannot get through.

How does hot water help open a jar?

Sometimes the cover or lid of a jar is so tight that you cannot open it. When you hold the lid of the jar under hot water, the lid gets larger, or expands. You cannot see the lid expand, but the lid gets looser. Soon you can turn the lid and open the jar.

What are Gypsies?

Gypsies are a wandering people. More than a thousand years ago, they left India. Since then they have spread over much of the world. In England, long ago, they were called Egyptians because some of them came from Egypt. Later the word Egyptian was shortened to Gypsy.

Although they live in many countries, the Gypsies keep their own customs and live together in family groups, or tribes. They have their own language, called Romany. No matter what country they live in, they call their own leader their king or queen.

Gypsies rarely stay long in one place. They are always moving on. Once they traveled in vans, pulled by horses. Today their vans may be trucks or trailers. When the Gypsies find a good camping place, the vans, or caravan, gather together. Sometimes tents are put up. In the evening, the Gypsies build a campfire and sing and play music and dance.

Sometimes you see Gypsies at a fair. The women tell fortunes. The men may trade horses or sell metal jewelry they have made.

How did Halloween start?

Long, long ago in ancient Britain, the people held a harvest feast each autumn. They ate apples and pumpkins and corn and other good food that they had grown during the summer. They believed, too, that on that autumn night of October 31st, ghosts, goblins, and witches could appear. They built bonfires to scare them away.

Today we know that there are no ghosts or goblins or witches, but we like to pretend there are on Halloween. We dress up in scary costumes and light pumpkin Jack o' Lanterns, and it is fun!

Are black cats unlucky?

You know that your purring little black kitten is not unlucky. No black cat is unlucky. Long ago people believed there really were witches and that a witch had a black cat. That was why they thought a black cat was unlucky. Today we know that there are no witches. We know no cat, no matter what his color, is unlucky.

What are fairies, elves, brownies, leprechauns, trolls?

Once upon a time some people believed there really were magical little people who could work charms and spells. Today we know these little people are not real, but live only in fairy and folk tales. This is what the fairy tales tell us about them.

A fairy is so tiny she can ride a butterfly. She has gauzy wings and a magic wand. There are good fairies and bad fairies.

A tiny elf lives underground. If you are near an elf hill, you may hear faint, elfin music because elves like to dance.

Brownies often live near Scottish farms. If you leave a bowl of milk behind a door for the brownie to drink, he will clean your house. But if there is no milk, he may make mischief.

A leprechaun is an Irish fairy shoemaker. If you catch a leprechaun, try to make him tell you where he has hidden the pot of gold all leprechauns have. But you must be clever because he is very tricky.

A troll hates the sunlight. He lives under a bridge or in a dark forest or underground. He knows how to mine gold and silver and precious jewels from the earth.

What is an echo?

If you stand on a mountaintop and call your name, you may hear your name called back to you.

Long ago in ancient Greece, some people thought that the call came from a mountain fairy called Echo. We know this is not true.

When you call your name from a mountaintop, the sound waves of your voice may strike the solid surface of a cliff or steep hill. Then the sound bounces back to you, and you hear your voice a second time. We call this an echo. You can hear an echo whenever sound waves strike a solid surface and bounce back.

Are there really mermaids?

There are no mermaids, but long ago sailors did believe that mermaids and mermen lived in palaces under the sea. A mermaid, they thought, had the body of a woman and a tail like a fish. Sometimes she sat on a rock and looked into a golden mirror as she combed her long, pale hair. Why did they believe in mermaids? The seal and the sea cow both hold their babies as a human mother does. If you saw one of those sea animals from far away, maybe you would believe in mermaids, too!

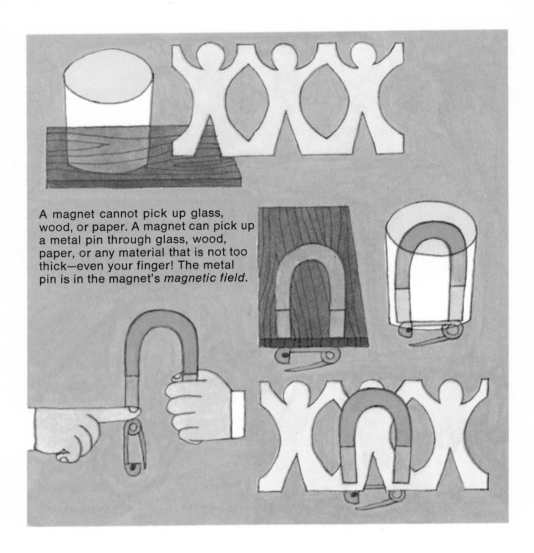

A magnet cannot pick up glass, wood, or paper. A magnet can pick up a metal pin through glass, wood, paper, or any material that is not too thick—even your finger! The metal pin is in the magnet's *magnetic field*.

How does a magnet work?

Usually a magnet is made of iron or steel. Steel is a very pure iron. A magnet may be shaped like a horseshoe or a bar. It can pick up a metal pin or an iron nail. It cannot pick up glass, wood, or paper.

A magnet has two poles. One is called the north pole. The other is called the south pole. If the north pole of one magnet swings toward the north pole of another magnet, the two poles push each other away, or repel each other. This happens with the two south poles, too. But if the north pole of a magnet swings toward the south pole of another magnet, the two poles pull toward each other, or attract each other.

Iron is made up of tiny particles, or molecules, of iron. In a magnet, the iron molecules line up and pull together. These lines are called the lines of force.

A metal pin has iron in it, too. When a magnet is near a pin, the iron in the magnet pulls, or attracts, the iron in the pin. The lines of force pull the opposite poles of the iron molecules in the magnet and pin toward each other. The space around a magnet in which it can pull a pin or other iron piece is called its magnetic field.

Glass, wood, and paper do not have iron in them. The iron in the magnet cannot pull, or attract, them.

What makes a compass work?

The earth is a giant magnet. It has a magnetic North Pole and South Pole. These are not in the same places as the geographic North and South Poles.

The compass needle is a little magnet. It points to the magnetic North Pole which pulls, or attracts, it. The geographic and the magnetic North Poles are not far apart. When a compass needle points north, it will guide you north to where you want to go.

North Pole

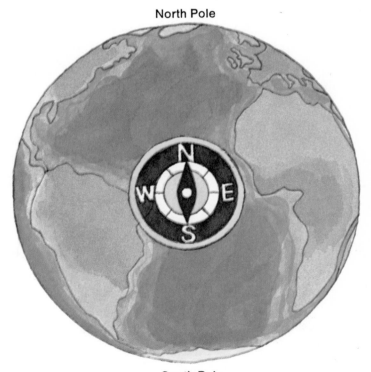

South Pole

What is a mirage?

Did you ever see a lake that wasn't really there? Sometimes you may see one on the desert. Sand is all around you, but there is a lake of shimmering water. As you come close to the lake, it moves away or perhaps disappears. It isn't a lake. It is a mirage.

A mirage is like a reflection in a mirror, but it is a reflection of light from the sky. The air over the desert is hot. If there is a layer of cool air just above the hot air, something happens. Light rays go straight through the cool air. They bend upward through hot air. When the light from the sky comes down, bends, and reaches your eyes, you see a reflection of the sky. It looks like shimmering water.

There are different kinds of mirages. Some make you see ships and land that are really far away. Some make you see upside-down trees and houses. But all mirages are caused by light rays going through layers of air of different temperatures.

Even though a mirage is not real, you can take pictures of it just as you can take pictures of a reflection in a mirror.

Why is ice slippery?

When you walk or skate on ice, your weight presses the bottom of your shoe or skate against the ice. This pressure makes the ice melt a little, and you slip. When you slip on ice, you rub against it and heat it. More ice melts. You slip faster and faster.

Why do some things get hot more quickly than others?
Sometimes you leave a scissors on a sunny window sill. When you come back later and pick up the scissors, it feels hot. If you touch the wood of the window sill, it does not feel as hot as the scissors. Yet the sun was shining on the scissors and the window sill at the same time. Why was the scissors hotter than the wooden sill?

The scissors is made of metal. Heat travels quickly through metal. The window sill is made of wood. Heat travels more slowly through wood.

How can heat travel through a scissors? All things on earth are made of tiny particles, called molecules. Molecules are always moving, but heat makes them move faster. When the sun's heat touches the scissors, the metal molecules begin to move faster and bump into the molecules next to them. They carry heat to those molecules and make them move faster, too, and bump into the next molecules. This keeps going on until all the molecules in the scissors are moving fast and carrying heat through the scissors. The scissors is hot.

Heat can travel faster through some materials, or substances, than through other substances. Heat travels quickly through metal. It travels more slowly through air, wood, glass, and other substances.

Why don't you try to experiment and find out which things in your house get hot quickest when you put them on a sunny window sill?

183

How can a magnifying glass make fire?

Did you ever do an experiment in school with a magnifying glass? Did you notice that the glass is thick in the middle and thin at the edges?

When light rays from the hot sun pass through this kind of glass, the rays are bent toward the middle of the glass. They gather together, or concentrate, in a point of light.

If a sheet of paper is placed so that this tiny dot of hot sunlight falls on it, the light rays gather at the point of the tiny dot. The paper usually catches fire, and it burns.

Why can't I see through a mirror?

You can see through a window. The light goes straight through the glass. A mirror is a glass with a coat of silver paint on its back. The paint stops the light and the light bounces back. We say that the light is reflected.

Look into a mirror. Do you see that everything is backwards? You lift your right hand. Your mirror reflection lifts its left hand.

When light bounces off you, into the mirror, and straight back again, your mirror shows you a backward reflection of yourself.

Water can act as a mirror, too!

What is the biggest thing there is?

The biggest things we know are giant red stars. They are millions and millions of times bigger than our sun. They are so huge that even though they are far, far away, they still can be seen shining in our sky. We do not know which red star is the biggest.

What is the greatest wonder in the world?

You are! You can ask questions. You can find answers.

Birds fly. Fish swim. They do what they were created to do.

A man does not have wings to fly, but he can fly in a plane. He does not have fins like a fish, but he can explore the ocean depths in machines. Only man can change the world around him to meet his needs. He is the only living thing on earth that has a human brain.

Once people laughed when men dreamed of flying or sending a rocket to the moon. Today many planes fly in the air. Rockets zoom into space. How did this happen? Somebody asked a question. Somebody found an answer.

You can ask questions. You can find answers, too.

Index

To make this index easy to use, entries are in alphabetical order, but sub-entries are in page number sequence. If you turn to Space Exploration, for example, under it you will find Space satellites, 121, 122, How spacecraft are launched, 123, etc.

An asterisk * indicates an illustration.